A Constellation of Kisses

Also by Diane Lockward

The Uneaten Carrots of Atonement
Temptation by Water
What Feeds Us
Eve's Red Dress

Greatest Hits: 1997 - 2010 (chapbook)
Against Perfection (chapbook)

The Practicing Poet: Writing Beyond the Basics
The Crafty Poet II: A Portable Workshop
The Crafty Poet: A Portable Workshop

The Doll Collection (anthology)

A Constellation of Kisses

edited by

Diane Lockward

Terrapin Books

Terrapin Books
4 Midvale Avenue
West Caldwell, NJ 07006

www.terrapinbooks.com

ISBN: 978-1-947896-17-8
LCCN: 2019904235

First Edition

Contents

With a kiss let us set out for an unknown world.

—Alfred de Musset

Foreword

A kiss is never just a kiss—heat-seeking, information bearing, coded. In this inspired collection, poet and editor Diane Lockward has assembled over 100 poems about kisses written by many of our best contemporary poets. You'll find kisses longed for, kisses auditioned, kisses rehearsed. Ritualistic kissing. Delicious kissing. Kissing that comforts the grieving. Kissing that blesses a union. Here's "that first kiss, / long as a river" in Tim Seibles' poem "Unmarked." And here comes the kiss of yearning in Susan Aizenberg's poem: "It's that kiss you want for so long // that when you take it you take it / greedy as a thief," an "epic" kiss, "a kiss worth whatever it costs."

Kisses in this anthology may be romantic or funny or comforting or erotic or mournful—and more. They're exchanged in any number of human combinations, and even between a woman and her nonhuman companion in Yvonne Zipter's delightful "Kissing the Long Face of a Greyhound." Kissing may be fleeting or remembered dimly. Or kissing may turn into the wonderful, lingering event of Ellen Bass's "Gate C22." Or consider Jennifer Burd's poem about a kiss in prison "so real that by the end of it, / the prisoner was a free man."

You'll find in this anthology kissing in many spots on the body and in other places, not all of them Paris. Rodin's *The Kiss* makes multiple appearances. As if there can never be enough, nearly as many "kisses" echo in Richard Jones's poem "Kisses" as there are lines in the poem.

This anthology even alerts us to what may be measured about kissing. Jane Ebihara informs us that kissing occurs between cows as well as snails, meerkats, puffins, and squirrels. She lets us know that "an average person kisses for a total // of two weeks in a lifetime." In "The Numerology of Kisses," Allison Joseph similarly engages in inspired counting: kissing "takes thirty-four muscles," and "the average woman kisses / seventy-nine men before she marries."

We may hope that kissing always begins in delight and keeps on being delightful. But the truth, of course, is otherwise. This is, after all, a constellation of kisses. There are poems in this anthology about deceptions, betrayals, and violence. Consider the poignance of Elya Braden's poem about a kissing contest in a fraternity. Tony Barnstone describes "a nightmare kiss, a wrong man kiss." In "Like Your Grandfather Kisses You," Jan Beatty writes about the horror of the abuse of children: "it was him. there. in the lobby. our gray kneesocks. our twirling young bodies. touching us." Or consider Debra Bruce's devastating "Just a Kiss Goodbye at the Airport."

As soon as I heard this anthology's title, I thought of the words Jimi Hendrix made famous: "Excuse me while I kiss the sky." These pages are constellated with all manner of kisses in all manner of patterns.

Dear reader, why not wish for everything? May there be no end to the most genuine kisses, the right kisses, the ones that are good and meant for us to savor. And while we're at it, let's wish for no end to poems about kissing.

—*Lee Upton*

"Thus in winter stands the lonely tree . . ."

—Edna St. Vincent Millay

and there's another woman from a Hopper painting
dejected on a single bed, or gazing at a shrub
where birds strung out on firethorn berries grub
for worms that rise despondent in the rain.
The rain is sickened by its endless fall;
the clouds, exhausted, struggle to recall
brief forms they took beneath the friendless stars
that vanish toward the bleak edge of the cosmos.
                              . . .Thus in the interstellar dust
ponders the lonely god, wondering who blew up Olympus.
You do not have to be lonely, wrote a poet, who lied,
but consoled a lot of doleful people. It's lonely at the top
but better than the bottom of the pileup.
Kiss me now, my tragic anodyne.

—Kim Addonizio

Love in the Age of Broken Constellations

In the planetarium,
the universe is everywhere.

The man who controls the stars
has pressed the wrong button

and the milky way spins
around the ceiling, across the viewing
chairs and onto the floor.

A girl holds hands with Orion.
She is the first to unbuckle his belt.

The universe has never been
so close, never been part of her skin.

Her boyfriend reaches over her shoulder,
Vega is under his fingernails.

She leans in to kiss him
and the room lightens.

Where there were hands, now
there is emptiness, where there were stars—

white paint returns, the bare curve
of the dome missing its verses.
And what remains—

a mural of the virgin praying
for darkness, a saint whispering

for night to circle again,
to land quietly in his lap.

—Kelli Russell Agodon

Kiss

And when the moment,
　like an overdue train bearing to us
　　someone loved and too long

　　　　gone, a train we've waited days
　　　and nights for, pacing the platform,
　　our pulses thrumming *when, when,*

arrives—the camera close up, lush
　sweep of strings, *adagio*, the light high key,
　　resplendent as the dew-rinsed,

　saturated, dizzyingly green panoramas
the cinematographer's mapped as Camelot—
　　　　the moment

we have waited for, with the lovers,
　since their first meeting, Guinevere crouched
　　among damp reeds, unafraid, despite

her torn dress, smiling as she watches—
　he's young, all muscle and wit, a man's
　　easy grace—smiling, too, despite the chain

　and mail-clad villains, the honed,
　　bloody swords, knight of girlhood's promise,
　　　you remember—that moment

　when the camera frames the kiss
　she's asked him, finally, for. They are not tender,
but open their mouths wide, so we think

of eating, their heads working,
    a kind of fever, love's other face—
        we recognize it, don't we? Lancelot,

the man, the archetypal *only, always,*
  we dreamt of as girls those rainy childhood
  afternoons, Kens and Barbies moving

  stiffly in our small hands, our mothers'
stolen stilettos gorgeously tripping us up.
It's that kiss you want for so long

    that when you take it you take it
  greedy as a thief and always with as much payment
due. And we want them to go on,

though we know the ending, that the camera
  must pan to a three-shot, Arthur's ragged
    face. We want them to go past

what they—and we—can bear, to follow
  his head gentle down her neck, her mouth
    against his bare shoulder. We want the music

  to swell, lavish, hokey, romance
engulfing us like some over-sweet perfume,

    so wholly our lives
  become epic, a kiss worth whatever it costs.

—*Susan Aizenberg*

A woman just wants to sleep

but her granddaughter wants her first *real* kiss. The woman watches her fantasize. She tries to tell her it's not all it's cracked up to be. Kissing, she means. The woman no longer cares for it. But the girl, whose name is Marta, is not convinced. The problem is, she's not alone. There's a whole party of adolescent girls in her bedroom, each one trying to kiss her own lips. The girls lean into the mirror, imagining, *What if?*

Darlings, the woman sighs, *it's just saliva, tongues, ick.* But then she has to admit, she's the adult, but she sounds like a kid. Maybe that's where the confusion lies. The girls giggle and ask each other, *Have you tried this?* They give each other Tic Tacs, lip gloss, and Teen Magazine, highlighting passages under *First Kiss Tips: Don't eat garlic, onions, or anything that causes belches, bad breath, or flatulence. Practice kissing the back of your hand first, then the mirror. Aim for the lips, cocking your head to one side so you don't bump noses.* But then the question arises, *To part or not to part the lips? If yes, how much?* The woman advises, *Just a slit. You don't want to appear too hungry. Remember, all the planning must appear to be his.* She's an old woman, after all. And not a feminist.

Yes, my girls, you want to appear a mere wisp, a hint, a wish, she continues. But soon they are asking, *What if he slides his tongue behind your teeth? What if, in a moment of anxiety, you bite him?*

This, of course, is a life and death question. *Bite him hard,* the woman says, but not out loud. Thinking about it, she can't sleep. She begins to feel a little hungry, even if it's been years since she's had an appetite. She listens as the girls whisper in the dark, as the night sails away like a kite with no string. When she finally sleeps, she dreams of eating a wet, bruised peach.

—Nin Andrews

Integration

Almost lost in his mouth. He'd told me I didn't know how to kiss, I was trying too hard, and showed me, so our mouths ripened to plush opening peonies, ruffling, even a bit messy at the edges. More than a mother's mouth, nipple, these kisses. Shape to shape, unforming and reshaping, play of inner cheek and tongue. My consonants: so crisp, he said. Every one of my syllables clear, enunciated. But this now was a time for vowels, color, the fibrous textures of slow diphthongs, blurred edges letting i's blend into u's, long e's open into ah, o, oh, oh, oh.

—Wendy Barker

Nightmare Kiss

The middle of a kiss, and though he opened
up wide and wider, her own small jawbones gave
a little *crack* and stuck, and look what happened:
as if she'd fallen in an open grave,
he swallowed her at last, and then she wandered
in a dark saturated country where
the red land throbbed with capillaries under
electric stars. A kiss had brought her there,
a simple kiss that rained and filled her head
with blood, a nightmare kiss, a wrong man kiss;
why had she kissed a man with such a mouth,
with such thick teeth and jaws, such tongue, instead
of kissing someone who would let her out,
kissing someone nicer, who ate less.

—*Tony Barnstone*

Frida with Monkey

You wear heat like another layer of embroidered finery. It has scent, your heat, of jonquils and lime, of spices seared in a hot black pan. On your face blooms a flush of scarlet poppies. Oh, Frida, that face. Who would dare to paint that face? Half woman, half man. A nimbus of eyebrow. Your moustache drawn hair by hair. Scarlet, again, on your mouth. You could lay those lips on the monkey, guarding you, a part of you, twined together, its pelt your hair, paws enormous as a man's hands. In a moment you'll turn your head, and it will turn its head, drawn to your desire, the kiss.

—*Tina Barry*

Gate C22

At gate C22 in the Portland airport
a man in a broad-band leather hat kissed
a woman arriving from Orange County.
They kissed and kissed and kissed. Long after
the other passengers clicked the handles of their carry-ons
and wheeled briskly toward short-term parking,
the couple stood there, arms wrapped around each other
like he'd just staggered off the boat at Ellis Island,
like she'd been released at last from ICU, snapped
out of a coma, survived bone cancer, made it down
from Annapurna in only the clothes she was wearing.

Neither of them was young. His beard was gray.
She carried a few extra pounds you could imagine
her saying she had to lose. But they kissed lavish
kisses like the ocean in the early morning,
the way it gathers and swells, sucking
each rock under, swallowing it
again and again. We were all watching—
passengers waiting for the delayed flight
to San Jose, the stewardesses, the pilots,
the aproned woman icing Cinnabons, the man selling
sunglasses. We couldn't look away. We could
taste the kisses crushed in our mouths.

But the best part was his face. When he drew back
and looked at her, his smile soft with wonder, almost
as though he were a mother still open from giving birth,
as your mother must have looked at you, no matter

what happened after—if she beat you or left you or
you're lonely now—you once lay there, the vernix
not yet wiped off, and someone gazed at you
as if you were the first sunrise seen from the Earth.
The whole wing of the airport hushed,
all of us trying to slip into that woman's middle-aged body,
her plaid Bermuda shorts, sleeveless blouse, glasses,
little gold hoop earrings, tilting our heads up.

—*Ellen Bass*

Strategy of a Kiss

Begin at hinge, not lipped. Lidded. Outer canthus.

Ascend to eyebrow. A gentle press. Dry.

Arc to lacrimal duct. Don't rush. Laparoscopic
tongue, blindly.

The nostril curve. Don't linger.

Earlobe like an artichoke leaf. Savor.

The jawlined jugular. Fingertips can place
the pulse, the heat. Rest your lips. Regress.

Revive for clavicle. Slide

                              to sternum. Trap
breath and wait for condensation.

Nipple can be tricked, cajoled. Take between
your lips and cast a mold, a certain fit,
a memory.

The inside of elbow to wrist.

Bite middle knuckles, suck each fingertip, exhale
across palm so breath skims over the edge like falls. Drag
lower lip like the forgotten barrel.

Change your angle. Shoulder blades and sharper tongue.
Exact perimeters.

A railway of vertebrae, the concave links. Ride syncopation,
pulsely.

Two shallow dimples at the small of back, the span
between—pastry. Give a little sugar, little glaze, a drizzle
down the side.

Waist requires geometry and focus. Estimate trajectory
of abdomen. Aim for navel. No puckering.

Pace the thigh but take no shortcuts to the ankle.
The calf is no Kansas highway. Horizon,
a field of sweet corn. Graze.

Skim the metatarsal fan like swallows on a wire.

Strand yourself at toes. Beached. Reach for the water
sweating rings on the nightstand.

Repeat it all, reversed.

Repeat.

—*Michele Battiste*

Ariadne Invites Dionysius to Kiss Her

I know one of the Maenads
gave you a massage today—

I know you're eating chocolate cake
that may be better than sex.

Come over here
with that chocolate in your mouth

and let me kiss you, Dionysius—
let's kiss with our mouths open!

—*Jane Beal*

Like Your Grandfather Kisses You

flurry. morning flurry of the young. boys in green ties. girls in gray
plaid jumpers, running. to catholic school, then the scream. the dash.
race to the glass door. the scream & the dash. race to the glass door of
the foyer. (green tile lobby of the suburban school). girls sprinting full
out to beat the boys. no stopping before the red brick. learning. we
can't beat them. really beat them. but this first year of many. wild
mornings, all of us laughing in bunches. & crowding around him each
day the same. flurry. young children. waiting to be swooped up.
(waiting to be thought of). held too tight, youngness. held too
long, kissed. the patting & hair stroking. I am his favorite. like your
grandfather kisses you. he loves my oblivion. to his hands. he says.
he likes my smile. my 20 years before the charges are brought. my
smallness. priest. stands in his black cassock. next to the list of movies.
we are forbidden to see. by the holy statue. he swings us around. in his
finery. (next to the six ft. thermometer showing how hot). the chart of
the money we raised. how close we are. to our goal. for the christian
children's fund. it was him. there. in the lobby. our gray kneesocks.
our twirling young bodies. touching us.

—*Jan Beatty*

Good Nothing and Good Night

Whenever I pass a house under construction—open
frame squared on its foundation—I'm thrown back

to my first adult embrace, to a bitter January day,
old snow tattering the mounds around the site, drum

echo of our boots on raw planks, evening's first grays
pouring through the unclosed roof, had we paused

to look up or out. Trespassing, which carried its own
modest thrill (though no one cared about these

nascent suburban properties), we stood chilled at
the brink of fourteen, as I calculate now, yet how

serious I felt, and sincerely wooed, while sensing
the way the world was already closing in on us

as those walls soon would to complete a space
deemed inhabitable, but that dusk our mouths

nearly froze together, our coats bulky, our breaths
mist, and the framed-out doorway meant

little to us who walked through walls at will
content with the nothing we stepped

out to and the nowhere we were headed.

—*Jeanne Marie Beaumont*

Last Instructions for Evening

Hunger breaks windows, spins hailstones in the cold
heart's kitchen, nerves taut as a new-killed lamb.
Hunger, breadbox of old crusts. Bitter-tongued
drum-solo under the bed.
It wants to cry, it wants to kiss, but pride says *don't,*
its body twists for a skin-stripped naked
maestro,   no leftovers,   no bland rice.

Feed me slow cooking. Grasp my waist
supple with proposal, wake my mouth with
fresh cayenne, small ripe figs,
the white moth's kiss.
Say my name, please, call it an *amuse bouche.*
Don't forget a sauce stirred with wingtips
the color of God's sweet lips. The color of

darling! The color of *yes.* Bathe us,
first with warm cloths, then perfume
—to taste. Don't forget.
Feed me love, my love. Feed me caress.
Feed me a man cooked to perfection, basted with
our bodies' spring sweat, flavored with
tears sung in orgasm's slow low note, and laughter's

high. Simmer all the mute night by desire,
feed from fingertips dipped in the widow's
champagne. End, with a well-aged Armagnac.

This second birth.
Now, my love, light the hearth.
Burn the forest of appetite, kiss,
and   bless the food.

—Margo Berdeshevsky

First Kiss

Rag of memory pulled from the dirty basket,
temple youth group, kibbutz
close enough to the border
we could hear the Arab market,
back when border was a simple fact.
A wedding that night, streamers,
lights in the trees.
I hadn't been drinking but others
must have been. It happened
that a soldier I'd seen at the pool—
one was different than the rest,
tenderhearted,
that was not the one who liked me.
Our parents had paid to have us experience,
all summer that word, an *experience*
weeding fields peeling potatoes.
The soldier took my hand,
led me to his room.
Quick look around before
he turned out the light. You can't
imagine how dark,
full dark, the darkest part of dark.
Then we were on the bed,
was there anywhere else to sit?
His mouth on mine, and quick,
his finger inside me, only I didn't know
finger or that other?
I was very still trying to figure out.
Finger I decided, but maybe

more than one, and go ahead ask
why I stayed still, why I stayed,
ask if any part of me wanted.
I know it sounds absurd but I stayed
because I couldn't figure out
how to leave. I don't know
how long before I did figure out
one leaves by standing up and walking
to the door unless one is prevented
first by words and then by a hand.
But no, in this story I was not prevented.
Outside I didn't run, no need.
I walked back and saw my friend from the temple,
left her thinking whatever she was thinking
because I had no idea, not the first word,
and if the lights were still glowing in the trees
they guided me, and if not, I found
my way back in the dark.

I wonder now if my soldier,
can I claim him,
pin him to the flannel of memory,
wonder if he'd killed,
he couldn't have been more than eighteen,
and if he'd killed if all he could do
was drown his fingers
in the never-been-touched lake of me,
my contribution to the war.
Perhaps my soldier was dead by twenty.
I should stand on his grave and thank him
for not forcing. He must

have been still a boy the night
of streamers trailing and the lights
like eyes in the trees,
and I a small square of safety to stand on.

—Jacqueline Berger

They Are Kissing, in the Pub, Under One

They are kissing, in the pub, under one
dim bulb, cockeyed roof, starry pit of sky's
imperfect pearls, glint from the moon's glum
mouth, kissing. Kissing as the drained glass dries,
planets jig and reel away, urns are filled
and the columbine snakes its fragrance around
the mysterious hearts of youth. Hear her hip's
slender bell strike and clap, his chest pound,
the bone blade sound, when they are kissing.
Bodies long to break out, drag the mourning coat
behind—a lap dance among the living
as night scatters leaves down Aberfan Road.
Let them drink, taste the flesh they love and miss.
Let them honor the dead like that. Let them kiss.

—*Michelle Bitting*

Eiffel Tower: First Time

Do not the laws of natural forces always
conform to the secret laws of harmony?
—Gustave Eiffel

Twenty hours into the day and we land in Paris.
We run streets, stop for maps, turn ourselves
until we find it. At last, under the girders and lines

I spin, my arms out, all the years I have written
myself here converge. I release. My voice
sparks the air and its points: *Paris! Paris!*

My arms are a clock, broken from winding,
my numbers drop, unriveted for this moment
outside time. And I run to you. I want

you to lose me under this four-cornered
monument, this unreal iron dream made tangible,
to take my body and snap its boundaries

but you hold me without kissing back, tell me
not here, not now. And I shift myself into a pause
I do not want, wait to break our embrace.

We start to walk the gravel. I fall behind.
I stop and turn back, look up to the steeled shock,
the proclamation once temporary, now iconic.

When you see that I do not follow, you turn
to ask why. I say better to see the light.
My hands are a steeple beneath my chin.

Husband, do I will you to be who you cannot?
A man who kisses away the years we'd forgotten
in each other, a man whose lips press
the breath from me, whose intensity

is pointed heavenward, who collapses
with me on the grass and thinks nothing of other eyes,
only the drowning and baptism of our bodies?

I want you to make us
new again, as in our first kiss
from so long ago, my glass so full.

You return to stand quietly behind me.
You tell me we are older now.
Your hands find my waist.
I know you want to go.

But somehow
it all seems monumental.

Can I love you in this,
the way that you give?

Can I forgive
that there may never be more?

—*Julie E. Bloemeke*

After Your Shower,

that one drop, caught in a curl
        behind your ear
                swells, quivers &
        falls—
a tiny tear on your naked shoulder,
        rolls
        down
                sideways,
speeds along the inverted crescent of the scapula,
        along the brief tension of a muscle
                (you're shaving,
                every surface of your back moves)
then
        slows
down,
& ambles along
                your
                spine,
&, because I'm looking only
        at that tiny transparency,
                I shiver when it suddenly
        sucks up another drop,
plumps,
        swells,
                & quavers now,
buxom & boorish toward your loins.

Can't you feel that? Doesn't it tease
                as it lasciviously flows
toward where your buttock rounds, &—
                quick!—
                        now,
                                before it slips
        into that moist fold,   I crouch,
                                catch it
                with the hard,
upcurled tip of my tongue, &
                kiss you. Right there.

                —*Laure-Anne Bosselaar*

Winning Kiss

I won a fraternity kissing contest
in college. I still have the photo—
chubby dumpling me, squeezed
into too-tight jeans, perched
on a strange boy's lap. He
is blindfolded and I am holding
his face, leaning in. I never
thought I'd win. Too worried
about the heft of me on those boys'
laps to imagine they'd respond
to the ripeness of my lips,
the stealthy inquiries of my tongue,
my breath reduced to tiny sighs.

Why did my sorority sisters offer me up?
Did my six-month relationship
with a grad student who resembled
Warren Beatty credential me as
experienced? Or was it,
in the wake of our break-up,
now two months past, the wreckage
of clear-cut forest behind my eyes,
or the daily widening of my abundant hips
that bespoke a hunger so impersonal
that any lips would do?

—*Elya Braden*

First Acceptance

When the poet places the pistol to his temple,
it isn't the fifty-six meaningless jobs he has lost

or the four women who have divorced him
that flash before his eyes in protracted moments.

Flashing first are phrases like *after careful
consideration, unfortunately, we regret, going*

*to pass, not quite right for us, unable to meet
our current needs.* Then the poet is a boy

on the farm, hitting rocks out of the driveway
into a sunless sky, with a thin yellow bat he kept

for thirty-six years because his dad gave it to him
before driving away. Driveway dust swelled

behind tires and a tailgate, drifted with the wind
and disappeared. The boy was twelve when Kate

not only accepted his date, she made the first move
in Coulter's basement, the tip of her nose cold

on his neck, under his jaw, his cheek, his temple,
each kiss telling him to submit without question.

—*Jason Lee Brown*

The Kiss

for Laure-Anne

That kiss I failed to give you.
How can you forgive me?
The kiss I would have spent on you is still
there, within me. It will probably die there.
But it will be the last of me to die.

—*Kurt Brown*

Just a Kiss Goodbye at the Airport

She sees it happening and lets out a yelp—
Dad! His mouth is on her roommate's mouth,
her new best friend brought home for winter break.
So much alike, they've worn each other's clothes,

permission understood—both pear-shaped,
getting ready and talking in the mirror.
When one told about an uncle who snapped
the strap on her first bra, didn't the other

feel her own skin sting between
her shoulder blades as if she were still ten,
the oak's rough bark she'd pressed her back against
to scrape away his touch?

                                    An airport cop
whistles the father out of his parking space.
Neither girl can look at the other's face.
A blast of emptiness, a van pulls up,
boys their own age with backpacks tumble out.

—Debra Bruce

Prison Literature Class

Like the pages of their rented textbooks,
each student carries himself inside
a private, portable container
to protect his skin
from the walls of this place.

*

They bow their heads to the exam
I've given them on *The Importance
of Being Earnest* while spring killdeer cry
beyond the window cracked
to release the captive air.

Although they know I know their names,
each adds his number to every sheet,
double proof of identity:
once from the outside in
twice from the inside out.

*

I give them *home*work assignments
and take-*home* quizzes
and they all pass
even though that is never
where they do them.

*

They tell me they've got nothing but time,
and they serve it—the movement
of their blood doling out seconds and years
while they learn a new trade:
making pages from hours and walls.

In their weekly journal they all write
about the things they miss—the women
and men, the children they want to have
give them another chance,
the dreams they know they had
last night, which now escape them.

One writes about the walls he walks
inside these walls inside himself
and how something in him
does not love them
and something in him
cannot bear to bring them down.

Another writes a poem about a kiss
between an inmate and his visitor—
a kiss that everyone witnessed,
even the guards. It was a kiss so long
and so real that by the end of it,
the prisoner was a free man.

—*Jennifer Burd*

Panic at John Baldessari's Kiss

The aftermath always happening like an airplane falling, or a man
mid-air falling from a horse, and an arrow, a gun, many guns
pointing away, at us, our all bulls-eye-on-the-mark. This is what he
sees when he sees. Maybe *Wrong* or not, the appropriation, the film
clip, chase, pressed lips over lips, photo moment on the minute-drawn
breath in, the over, the under, bodies in black and white cut to pose,
the way a kiss can pose, dispose of everything around it for another,
dispose of thinking. It's like waving goodbye. Mouth to mouth seeing
as saying. Inside. Resuscitation back to the brain saying *yes* as the mouth
makes an O. Circles for the digital age, colored dots for faces already
made for erasing. Hurry, come, he, 6'7", sees fifteen minutes from the
Mexican border, cremates his old paintings up close. But the ashes were
kept in a book-urn, not so afloat in the ocean with my parents, *Above, On
and Under (with Mermaid)* to kiss and kiss, riot in the dark depth of it.
The collision, the kiss, the capture, once in the for-all-we-know of
haunting who comes first. Kiss into kiss and so into kiss. All laws
of gravity leave us. Gender begins in violence and space. Space begins
in gender and violence as all laws of gravity leave us. So, kiss, kiss, kiss!

—Elena Karina Byrne

Snow Day

Today, snow gloved the trees like a city of hands.
We shoveled to find the end of the world, shaking junipers

until their powdery pollen flickered
and fell on our heads. We dug out a canyon, a lacuna.

Entered the sky through a door of dirt-gristled snow
and the clock said there were hours.

The floor of the earth told secrets
so we put our ears to the manuscript of dirt and listened
as the lips of the world read us their sources.

I heard you whisper *thanks*
to my millions of cells. In an extended silence, you kissed me

in the oddest places: my right hip, above my fractured
coccyx, on my heels—
the parts of my body that go unnoticed.

Heaven can be generous. It gave us space to push
so I pushed against you and heard

what was not audible: bird tracks against white
and white moonlight:
the trance of memory, body, double-edged need.

We returned to light stroke and spread and leaned in;
inside we hardly knew what we'd left.

We rested in the method of finding our way
one limb at a time. The day tolerated our searching.

Insulated with dilating dark, we soaked
in each other as snow existed in another dimension.

After a while, when we saw only straight again,
we emerged with the capacity for endurance.
Snow stacked over us a little taller.

That's what happened: we were sweeping ice
from the footprints
when we fell into something crystalline: a sort of perfection.

—*Lauren Camp*

Birth of a Kiss

Thinking about the kiss I am about
to give birth to, I picture
my unborn kisses, like butterflies,
resting deep inside
the womb of kisses. A cave,
my body houses them. They
line up, waiting their turn,
watching my life unfold
on a big screen. They wonder
what kind of kiss they will be:
the kiss I give to my daughter,
my son; kiss on my mother's
soft cheek; kiss on the wet nose
of my cat. Each hopes, though,
to be the kiss that collides with
another kiss through the tunnel
of lips: the kiss between lovers
that lasts long with tongues
and nostrils flaring. They watch
me sneaking up behind my wife
who leans against the sink
rinsing dishes. I touch her waist-
length blond hair. She turns as the
screen flashes the countdown—
3-2-1, and the kiss flutters up
and up traveling from the center
of my belly through the diaphragm
and throat along filaments which no
scientist has ever been able to find

and enters the hard flower
of my mouth as her kiss does the same.
I feel all the unborn kisses still
watching, politely clapping but
secretly jealous as when we clap
for the winner whose name is drawn
from the raffle jar, thinking,
Lucky bastard, how come I never win?

                                    —*Neil Carpathios*

Aubade to My Husband

Through venetians,
sunrise seeps.
You're still

asleep, cradled
forehead between
right forefinger and thumb.

You look deep
in thought,
those eyes

dreaming of blue
dasher dragonflies
flitting in tall grass.

Cheeks orbed,
like the sun
is nestled inside.

Your lips—
the top, cusped peaks,
a channel chiseled in the middle,

the bottom, curled,
like a tulip petal,
arched just enough

to reveal a pink ledge
and thin crease
a ray could spill over

(like rain
rolling down
the mid-rib of a leaf).

Pursed, they are
withholding your dawn,
you still sleep.

I listen—
your heavy breaths—
and wish—

you awake, quietly
nudging
apart your lips.

—*Robin Rosen Chang*

Growing a Giant

My son stands on the counter
Asks to smell all of the spices.
They say he is small for his age.
I hate that
We are supposed to grow a giant,
That I am a failure,
That my womb,
My womanhood
Is the evitable culprit
Of any errors in his DNA.
Pair this with a Roman father
And police-officer mother-in-law
Who has grown a man
With *mani d'oro*
Golden hands.
They want him
To have an oxtail
As a pacifier
To lift baby weights
To yank his legs
To elongate them.
I, instead, grow him
One sweet kiss & embrace
At a time, another way
He can face the world
In strength. I hold him
On the counter, let him
Smell all of the spices:
Sweet basil, deep pepper,

Spicy chile flake, earthy bay leaf,
Tangy fennel, tart garlic.
I see him growing.
I am watching, can hear
The slow extension of love
Settling with the calcium
In his bones. I imagine
That is how everything begins,
With careful attention.
I imagine his healthy heart,
His strong hands of gold.

—Amanda Chiado

It's Something People in Love Do

*We were happy and wretched and cloudy
and setting fire to everything for warmth.*
   —Heather Christle, "Taxonomy of That November"

It's a late film, not one of their best, clogged
with a love interest that never really makes
your pants itch, but when the Marx Brothers
keep the train moving so the hero can make it
to town to record the deed and afford to marry
the girl of his dreams, they chop the whole
damn train up to feed the fire. Frightened
passengers in bustles and waistcoats watch
their seats axed from beneath them as women
cradle their children and men stand around
looking affronted. Then they hack up the walls
and the roofs, carrying armfuls of train forward
to turn into steam to keep things moving and
I'm not saying we should watch fewer old movies.
What I am saying is maybe everything's not
a metaphor for trying to pay the bills on time.
I love your credit score. It could pin my credit score
to the late summer soil and pee on its head.
My credit score would roll over and take it.
But what do you think of that chicken dinner
I made last night, how caramelized the thighs,
the bourbon from a plastic jug. How beautiful
that farmhouse looks passing by in the distance.
If we could get off this train we could go get it
and tear it to pieces with our teeth, tossing

hallways and lintels to the flames. Then we
could clean each other's face with our tongues.
It's called kissing. People in love do it.

—*Christopher Citro*

French Kiss

Sue Walbridge asked me if I'd ever
been kissed, ever had a French kiss.

Girls' locker room at Gray Junior High,
the beat throbbed from gym music

and the whole scene's crimson sweater sets,
the teased-up hair. One girl leaned into herself

to redraw kohl-dark eyes after a long jag
of vomiting and crying over the bear-hug

slow dance of her best friend with her man.
Never been kissed, I finally admitted,

and next I saw Sue's hand offering an orange
spiked with vodka, and bitter juice

filled my mouth. *For courage,* she said.
On Oakes Street, night after night, I rode

curious waves to sleep. What I imagined was pure
film and all 1940s—the smoldering looks,

a man who stalked closer and closer before
an embrace, and then the woman's gloved hand

which he began to kiss, and kiss, going up,
up the arm, above the elbow-length glove,

certainly, to the fine clavicle where—he stopped,
I guessed. Trying to crack the riddle of what

happened next or who said what, I smooched
my own hand and wrist in bed. You might

strip things down to this—ignorance and the shock
of its departure. Sue's later critique of her beau's

kissing said a lot, it's true, about tongues,
saliva, salt, but I never imagined my mouth

opening like that. After my first chaste kiss
exchanged in a car with Merle Thayne

while his father drove us home from a movie,
it was some sweet affirmation to find

my mouth pushed wide by another boy.
What a paradox of moisture, lips, heat,

and a glimpse of a landscape that seemed
both familiar and new. I've forgotten his name.

—*Patricia Clark*

Covered in Hickies

It's a primitive love ritual, reverse osmosis,
a filthy instinct we have to lock
our lips to any old skin and not let go.
The power of the peck. That one touch
that makes fathers weep, virgins blush,
politicians declare war. The no-fail motive
behind open condoms, broken hymens,
pro-choice, prison terms, same sex protests,
even Pretty Woman got down on her knees
just to avoid one kiss.

A lousy kisser is a neck biter, a Hoover,
the Red Sea, an easy lay—
tongue a temporary stop like a knocked door
or bags through an x-ray machine,
is divorce and bitter unease,
a lonely Saturday night and old movies—
watching him kiss her to color,
your own dull thumb locked on rewind.

But if you're good, you're Häagen-Dazs,
you're Zorro, that fantastical face in a pillow,
that scene from *Here to Eternity*—the force field
pull, the deepening, closed eyes rolling back,
the whole mouth an open airlock
on Mars and all the life being sucked
into that arid red desert,
feet ripping out of boots like a blast of Bolero,

everything else inside building, moving,
shifting, rushing to thunder,
the hurricane night deaf as a backdrop,

the night air sweet as nicotine.

—Cathryn Cofell

Whirring Journey

Two hummingbirds soared across the book's page.
We stood stunned, at the brightly colored maze—

two beaks caught, four wings whirring in bliss.
Swift against the twining, your hand touched the page

then brushed mine. *Feed the winged one honey, feed it loss.*
I remember a kiss after you stroked the ivory page.

Near a dusty museum shop on a side street,
we lingered, touching. Page after page

of splendid mornings turned to luxurious noon.
There's comfort in returning to this distant stage,

my name now an autumn berry suspended
from your lips, fire on a glittering page.

—*Geraldine Connolly*

The Temperature Reaches 102

The North Pole is melting,
and Antarctica, and in Greenland
glaciers break away—
my own small garden fills
with black rain and the scent of mud
and fermentation, heavy aromas
from long ago: I'm a feverish child
at the top of the stairs, dreaming
my mother in the room below,
hearing the shush of her slippers
and a metallic ping—ice
in her glass or the clasp to the door
she opens wide enough to let the night
whoosh in. I'm asleep
but awake enough to see her sway—
a liquid dance with the wind—
and the wind becomes a phantom
made of whiskey and steam.
Through drowsy eyes I see her
roll back her head and open her mouth
to drink him in, and I hear an owl
in my throat—I'm trying to cry Stop,
but why should my mother
listen to me now?
She's a lipstick smudge,
a thirsty moan, a floe
wanting nothing from life
but to melt. I press my own mouth
against the wall and dream

of breaking levees, houses that drift
out to sea—plaster damp
with the phantom's scent. My eyes
are closed, yet I see him plume
across my world, dark and bright
as oil. He'll kill my mother first,
and then my knees will bend—
in the end, I'll marry him.
I know this even after the wind dies down
and I wake a grown woman,
flushed and queasy but safe
in a sun-drenched room,
every window and door
latched tight.

—*Jackie Craven*

Tongue, No Tongue

My Uncle Steve died at 86 after falling
one time too many in Parkinson's slow
agonizing descent. Maybe everybody
mostly half-relieved—though my mother,
his older sister, I'm not speaking for.

She's legally blind and three-quarters deaf.
Her brother had been reduced to moving
his lips and imagining sound came out.
Their last heart-to-hearts were telepathic,
the soft light of his bedside vibrating

with the unspoken, the unheard.
They used to have dinner together
once a month until one day no one could
ever cook again. I simplify from this safe
distance, states and years away,

breaking my promise not to speak for her.
My mother on the phone gives herself
a pep talk while I listen, staring out
at the wind's bluster—at 89, she's said
goodbye to just about everyone, paid

her last respects so many times
that her brother is breaking her bank.
She tells me Uncle Steve once
asked her to show him how to kiss
when they were 17,18—a little old

for that? Maybe her timing's off—
she agreed, but told him *no tongue.*
My mother has never mentioned
French kissing to me in any context
in my 60 years. Uh-huh, I say,

and she's off with more tongue tales:
my brother kissing his wife
and my mother could see the tongue
and she didn't think it was right
to do that in front of his mother!

I am trying and not trying to visualize
the kissing lesson—standing, sitting,
lying down? Its duration, completion,
the tenor in the room, and what made
my mother the expert? She presses

a wrong button, and our connection
is lost. Did the light vibrate
with the unspoken?

—*Jim Daniels*

Revisiting the Psalms

Oh, David, your question about poetry
sent me scurrying to my books
when I should have been dusting
the shelves and baking quiche
for the New Year's party
to which I am sure I have invited
more people than my house will hold,
rather, my apartment, but you asked
about poems, poems by Jewish poets
about poetry. The term *ars poetica* isn't
Hebrew or Yiddish or Ladino, but
gave me an excuse to thumb through
Adrienne Rich and Alicia Ostriker,
from there to Gerald Stern, while thinking
he does not write about poetry,
but beauty. Are they the same thing?
Then Kunitz and his preoccupation
with time. I may spend the entire
day searching. My guests
will have to settle for mixed nuts
and Hershey's kisses. Not Ed Hirsch,
though he might have penned
an appropriate poem.
                    Before she married,
my grandma had a suitor
named Hirsch or Hersch, she often spoke
about. First name? Last name?
I don't know. Sometimes she called him
Hershey's Milk Chocolate, sometimes

Hershey's Kisses and spit him
in my grandpa's face during many
arguments. Who knows why
she did not marry Hersch?
She read so much *True Romance*,
then constantly bickered with grandpa.
Now I'm exploring poems
when I should be sweeping floors.
I never saw them kiss, not even
a peck on the cheek. Not even
when we watched the ball
drop on New Year's Eve.

—*Jessica de Koninck*

Exposed

You try not to bruise
the tangerine while you peel

back the pulp, mindful
how tearing into plumpy flesh

too quickly leaves you
wanting. You dangle a second

from its threaded vein—
the single crescent you will lift

to your mouth just before light
breaks, the night spent

kissing below the arc of the moon
causing you to question

how cold fruit must become
once you pull away the rind.

—Maureen Doallas

In Koine Greek

I can say *I loosen*, which also means
I forgive, and I can say
he is believing or *she is writing*
though I don't know whether she writes a list
of her father's virtues or directions
for boiling custard or a letter to her mother describing
how craggy light shadows these mountains at dusk.
My lover asks me to say *I love you*, but I have studied
only to lesson three. I don't know how
to say *I love you*, so I say *a heart speaks truth*.
Next week I will be able to say
a sister has words and *children*
hear a kingdom. They will imagine
trumpets, drums, clattering hoofbeats, a crier
to announce their arrival, the hush of velvet as he bows.
Now I say, *you hear a heart*
because I cannot say *I will kiss you* unless I skip
ahead, learn complicated inflections. I'm confident
our text will reveal conjugations of *kiss*, for Judas
kissed Jesus at least once, and I recall Paul
urging us to greet one another with a holy kiss. That's not
the kiss I want. I want a nuzzle, a snuggle, a smooch.
I can say *I desire* or *I wish*. I am hunting
for the verb *to smooch* but find it
nowhere. Has anyone ever smooched you
in Koine Greek? Has anyone ever said *heaven is kissing*
a sea or *earth is kissing glory*? I can say
heaven is knowing earth which I imagine
requires more than one kiss.

In Koine Greek, *you are loosening a kingdom,*
I hear a house of hearts, we are writing
heaven, where we will awaken
to loosen our limbs, to proclaim
O glorious verb!

—*Lynn Domina*

Cradle Thief

"A cradle thief," my mother called the man
we'd see in shops, cafes, parks, even church,
with "that poor girl" beside him. Hand in hand,
they'd walk as if they didn't feel the scorch
of people's stares. The day we saw him press
his lips to hers, my mother blocked my eyes
as if his mouth (I longed for my first kiss)
against her mouth was smothering her cries.
All week, I ran a fever that wouldn't break.
"A cradle thief"—a voice I only half
knew as my own surprised me in the dark,
my sick-bed wet with shivers. "A cradle thief,"
I said again, as if the words could will
my window broken, footprint on the sill.

—*Caitlin Doyle*

Kiss Me You Fool

When we were first dating
I bought you a pair of windup lips.
When you unwrapped them
from their tissue paper
you twirled the knob
on the back. The lips took
their obligatory waddle.
I laughed, and you laughed
an obligatory laugh,
then ignored the gift after that.
I promised myself I would never say this—
but I didn't like the way you kissed.
That seems petty now, after all
that's happened. I knew
if we got married I'd get used
to your tepid tongue, and I did.
Remember when I used to kiss you
hard? I was trying to teach you
how to kiss me. I suppose
you didn't like my kisses either—
why is she so aggressive?
you might have asked yourself.
Today I took the windup lips—
after sixteen years, they still worked—
and let them walk off the table,
a plastic suicide, a cartoon goodbye.
The gift I gave you was resilient.
It took quite a few tries before the legs
broke off, before the little knob
and spring slid across the floor, before
the hollow lifeless lips popped off.

—*Denise Duhamel*

Last Kiss

First, in your seventies and alone, you read that those who
count such things say an average person kisses for a total

of two weeks in a lifetime. And you realize your two weeks
was up some time ago. Suddenly there is kissing everywhere

you look. And you learn that cows kiss and squirrels. Puffins,
snails, and meerkats! And you are overcome with sorrow and

an overwhelming desire to kiss—to be kissed. And you learn
that's called *basorexia* and you have it. You watch the lips

of strangers in the supermarket—wonder if one would want
to kiss you. You know now that a minute of kissing burns

twenty-six calories and that a man lives up to five years
longer if he kisses his lover before he goes to work. You want

to tell someone that. And what's worse, unlike the first kiss,
the last slipped by unnoticed—unnoted. It might have been

a spring day when daffodils answered the sun's invitation or
an autumn day when everything else was burning. Or simply

a day you took out the garbage, did a load of wash. Then, someone
comes and takes your hand and you remember words

to a song you thought you'd never hear again and you remember
all those sunsets you forgot to watch and the smell of woods in rain.

And you remember the river, the river—how it presses
its mouth again and again to the swollen sea.

—*Jane Ebihara*

When I turned fourteen, my mother's sister took me to lunch and said:

soon you'll have breasts. They'll mushroom
on your smooth chest like land mines.

A boy will show up, a schoolmate, or the gardener's son.
Polecat around you. All brown-eyed persistence.

He'll be everything your parents hate, a smart aleck,
a dropout, a street racer on the midnight prowl.

Even your best friend will call him a loser.
But this boy will steal your reason, have you

writing his name inside a scarlet heart, entwined
with misplaced passion and a bungled first kiss.

He'll bivouac beneath your window, sweet-talk you
until you sneak out into his waiting complications.

Go ahead, tempt him with your newfound glamour.
Tumble into the backseat of his Ford at the top of Mulholland,

flushed with stardust, his mouth in a death-clamp on your nipple,
his worshipful fingers scatting sacraments on your skin.

Soon he will deceive you with your younger sister,
the girl who once loved you most in the world.

—*Alexis Rhone Fancher*

What I'm Good At, Sweetest Mama

Flute song rising like smoke from that 2 a.m. window,
October, the 1960's, San Francisco,
my fingertips tracing circles across my belly
as I listened—up to the heart and down, down,
they called it *effleurage* at the home for unwed mothers
and I thought it meant *flowering*. The sleeping city, the stranger,
his drowsy riff down the street somewhere—
in my bed where Jennifer Lisa ripened toward stillbirth,
I gathered joy with my fingers, stroked joy like petals
into a heap that was the mound of her, as she shifted, floated,
curved me, carved me. You were always afraid for my suffering.
Always afraid *of* my suffering. Now, on your trolley,
you're the queen, the silence; I stroke your hair, dare to kiss
your widow's peak, your lips, one last time I anoint you
with carnation cologne as I used to do when I'd visit,
three drops for you, three drops for me—
                                    What I do best,
I guess, is idolatry. When I caress you on the trolley,
beneath the sheet you are bone, your starved hands
and legs and pelvis already skeletal, your nose and cheekbones
arrogant. Once again I am gathering petals.
Like smoke the flutesong wanders toward oblivion.

                    —Ann Fisher-Wirth

Reading Boccaccio

A kissed mouth doesn't lose its freshness:
like the moon it turns up new again.

So says the *Decameron*, still teaching
after six hundred years. How many
mouths can one book inspire in six
centuries? A hundred a day if lips
are eager and the moon is shining.
Do the math. That's over twenty-two
million—Ohio and Illinois combined.
I say *Read.* With practice, you could
be the Johnny Appleseed of Kisses,
meandering the Midwest, knee-
deep in corn, perpetually puckered.
Who wouldn't greet you at the gate?
Clear a path through the fields
to reach one whose mouth turned up
fresh and new all the time?

When I was still fresh and new,
rising slender as a sliver each dawn
from my innocent bed, what did I know
of kisses before there was Kenny—
Picklehead my sister called him—
boy of loose limbs and red hair
who sang when we danced.
But the night he finally bent to me
and trotted out his kiss, what I got

was a rake of teeth, a hit-and-run
collision of the mouth. What I wanted
was to be ruined, to fling back my head
in an unbearable sweetness, what Boccaccio
must have known with his Fiammetta in the garden
at the end of the seventh story, second day.

—*Alice Friman*

Like Koi in Deep Water

That first kiss—
not sweeping one side
of the face then the other,

not a butterfly kiss, air kiss,
chocolate kiss. More than
spin the bottle bashful kiss.

His worn leather jacket
rolled into a pillow. His
soft hands, wide blue eyes.

Her speckled sea-green
pleated jumper, ruffled
blouse, pearl buttons.

The heavy scent of damp
trees, the oxygen rich air.
Two teens vowing forever.

His nicotine breath, the school
ring swinging like a fishing line
on a chain about her neck.

More like eager lips. Clumsy
tongues along lips' edges—
smacking, sputtering, splashing.

Lips gulping, slurping, sucking
stolen breaths of upstream-
freedom as the silver moon

turned its light switch on
and off. Something more like
cold-water kissing turned its

light switch on and off.
Something colder like
a slap across the face—

more like a swim in a lake.

—*Deborah Gerrish*

Eighteen

We never spoke of what my body
couldn't do, so when Jen and Kay
left to pick apricots from the spindly tree
behind the library, I hesitated.
But Rich would be there.
I showed up in a wraparound skirt,
my excuse to stand at the base,
pluck from the bottom branch.
The fruit was concentrated at the top.
While the others climbed, of course
it was Rich I watched, squinting
up at him as I had all summer.
The night before, he'd finally
kissed me, his tongue tentatively
grazing my own. *Catch*, he called
now and I lifted my skirt to form
a net, no thought to palsy, to exposing
my uneven legs. When the first
tangy oval dropped into the voile
I had already begun to taste it,
how it felt to be chosen. And whole.

—Ona Gritz

Eisenstaedt's Kiss

August 15, 1945

I dream for my parents it was just like this:
the anonymous sailor, the anonymous nurse,

her head in his arm, his hand at her waist,
on Times-Square that day in August

about when my father came down the ramp
and they kissed like those strangers I hope,

bending together, my mother and father,
curve into curve, these mythical lovers.

—Bruce Guernsey

The Kiss

My friend and I circle *The Kiss*, Rodin's
tribute to the lovers who were left, then caught
and killed for their failure to fail in
love. Look at the way they nearly resist
the embrace: their left arms not quite engaged,
her arm raised to encircle his shoulder and
his hand around but not resting, almost freed
from her hip. They sit close so ribs expanded
in breath must have let each body lean
to the other, and when breath began to coincide,
then each slipping to the space between
must have caused this kiss, my friend and I decide.
He stands on one side and I on the other.
Separate ends, a perfect diameter.

—*Tami Haaland*

Old Testament

You tell me
you are ruthless
and vengeful
as God.

Then you grab me
and kiss me
hard
on the lips.

I love God
I answer, tasting
the blood.

I say *God*
you look good
with your buttons
undone.

—*Jared Harél*

Temple

Not a place of worship exactly
but one I like to go back to
and where, you could say, I take
sanctuary: this smooth area
above the ear and around the corner
from your forehead, where your hair
is as silky as milkweed.
The way to feel its featheriness best
is with the lips. Though you
are going gray, right there
your hair is as soft as a girl's,
the two of us briefly young again
when I kiss your temple.

—Jeffrey Harrison

When Sex Was Kissing

In high school I was somehow able to kiss
for three hours continuously without consummation.
I still remember the underwater feel of the car,
how the windows steamed, the binnacle-glow
of the dash pointing us forward towards the trees,
the jerky light outside of a diver approaching
the wreck, pointing at this window, then that,
the policeman asking if we were okay. Sure
we were! The brake handle of the Renault
stuck up awkwardly between us. She wore
the scarab bracelet I'd given her, a pleated
white shirt with a gold circle pin plausibly said
to symbolize virginity, a green-blue plaid
wrap-around skirt closed by a huge safety pin,
and stockings held by garters. Only her Capezio flats
were shucked to the car floor. Deftly, she parried
my hands wandering under her skirt, her blouse,
while somehow welcoming my embrace.
Such fine diplomacy might have saved Poland!
I remember how each cubic inch of her was
agonizingly delightful, the soft hinges
at the back of her knees, her warm wrists touched
with Wind Song, the clean scent of her bubble-cut.
Every one of my cells awoke.
Finally, I went home bug-eyed, stunned,
half-drowned, and sat hours until dawn,
testicles aching—poor, haunted witnesses.

—*Hunt Hawkins*

Record

Ten years later, I can laugh
at how I started out dreading
the night I got my first French kiss,
laugh, too, at how nervous I was with my date, with myself,
how I didn't trust the chemistry
that crackled and burned between us like a lava flow,
how, when he smiled at me in the restaurant,
I had to stop my neck from swiveling
to make sure there wasn't a better, prettier woman behind me

But then, when I remember him driving me home,
I stop laughing and my body gets quiet and warm,
just like it did in his car after I made some corny joke
about love at first sight and he pulled into the driveway and said,
"It wasn't love at first sight, but I love you now."

And I remember his glance hot and soft
as a September sun on my face
and how I knew he was telling the truth,
our attraction so palpable not even my favorite
Mariah Carey remix playing on his car stereo
could distract me from it, and how my breath
seemed to get tangled in my lungs
but it didn't matter because suddenly his mouth
was on my mouth, my soul pulled into the pink suction
of his lips, my nose filled with the musk
and sandalwood scent of his cologne,
my awkwardness slipping away from me
like lingerie liberated in his hands

as he guided my hands to the muscles
beneath his respectable khaki shirt,
his tongue touching my tongue,
licking like a needle on a record,
patiently probing and circling as I licked him back,
my rigid black curves spinning and flaring
into a love song as primal and erotic
as the pulsing between my thighs

—*Shayla Hawkins*

Matilda Waltzing

My mother never expected it from a Yankee sailor:
He understood her Russian request, *Potseluy menya*
and acquiesced with a kiss,
in Australia, 1943.

Her immigrant father saw a fine partner
for his machine shop and daughter—
he didn't foresee her waltzing away.

Or, you might say she took a great leap

from New South Wales to the New World,
where her sailor waited after the war,
after their letters.

Michigan chilled the girl who'd never known snow,
though she warmed to his Slavic clan.
Their marriage, good and fruitful.

With five children grown, he gave her Florida,
the beach and salty sun,
bougainvillea to bring back her youth.

For sixty-six years, my mother has known
that she never would've said it in English.
Yet she'd dance their waltz again—

her sailor gone a decade now. She gets by alone
but longs for what's buried Down Under,
still sees her father standing below the gangway,
his hat filling with rain.

—*Karen Paul Holmes*

The Tiniest Toad in Moore County, NC

catches my eye, hopping with great care
over the rough flagstone. Don't spook her,

I think: if a toad springs from your path,
death is sure to follow. Never turn out

a toad at the threshold: the worst luck
will follow for a year. Finding the creature

in your home, remove it to nature
with kindness for witches possess them

as familiars. If you happen on a toad's dead body,
place it on an anthill until the flesh is eaten away.

Its bones that don't bob easy on water,
those you wrap in white linen and hang

in a corner to engender love. On a new moon,
if the bones float in a stream, they're charmed; slide

them into your pocket or hang them from your neck
'ere the devil gets them first. Then you can witch,

it's said and won't be witched yourself. She leaps
from stone near the fake frog pond's edge,

where the real frog eyes her with desire
from his tenuous perch on a lily pad.

She nestles under a leaf to hide her nudity.
Here in the poet's garden, she promises me

her tiny bones one day, a kiss for my civility.

—*John Hoppenthaler*

Satin Lips

First she exfoliates:
rubs granules of sea salt,
sloughs off the cracks and chap
of too much, or too little use.
Then she applies a slippery
lip balm: sticky Plumeria kisses
and mango wishes,
and waits for someone to notice
how soft she's become.
So sweet,
she smells of berry pears,
Madagascar vanilla, cherry
almond milk bath. Her hair
glistens with grapefruit elixir;
her face shimmers in mint
aloe cream, limbs polished
like wet leaves and citrus.
But her lips,
her *oooh* baby lips
are soft pillows of apricot
moistened just so.
Her lips pout, she knows
there's no doubt mouths will water.
Some boy ought to
just step up and pucker.

—*Karla Huston*

The Last of Our Embraces Transformed from the First

I see our skulls, our grave bones move
when we step toward one another to kiss,
the dry hard whiteness coming close even
as our lips touch and our jawbones drop
for our mouths, our tongues. And I hear
that low hiss from the other side where
no one we know knows the amazement
of our love, or how costly it's been to keep
and grow. I don't care that death stands inside
of life, or that your head and chin, without flesh,
are as real to me as your tongue, or that moist
rim of tenderness I see in your eyes. I call this
the great night that steps into and out of us
constantly, trying us on like garments, counting
the hours until we become its complete possession.
The mystery is not that we die, we know this, we
take it like fall coming on, or winter—the mystery
is that love opens us again and again, brings us
back to tenderness and holiness, back to marrow.

—*Gray Jacobik*

Kisses

Is there anything more sacred than a kiss?
At the marriage of true minds, a holy kiss
blessed by a priest seals the wedding vows
of the consecrated bride and groom, who,
with closed eyes, touch their lips together—
their kiss a sign of the life they begin as one.
For days, newlyweds do nothing but kiss,
a rudderless ship adrift on an ocean of bliss.
In time, their lives are defined by untold kisses:
good morning kisses, good night kisses, even
goodbye kisses, and then welcome home kisses,
followed by sweet days and nights of kisses.
All seasons prove perfect for knowing kisses.
Babies are born and showered with kisses
and the souls of children grow fat on kisses.
Meanwhile, the old married couple keep on
kissing until they can kiss no more. Together,
they go to heaven, where they are welcomed
by all the saints, who greet them with a kiss.

—*Richard Jones*

The Numerology of Kisses

To make a kiss, it takes thirty-four muscles,
abundant nerve endings in the lips but just
one bone, the lower jaw, sole moving bone
in the head. Who knows when humans

began to pucker, first felt that rush
of blood to the lips, surge in heart rate
and blood pressure, endorphins doing
their cha-cha in our brains? In a one-minute kiss,

you burn six calories, and scientists
speculate the average person, in a lifetime,
will spend over 20,000 minutes kissing—
over 120,000 calories burned, best diet ever.

The first filmed kiss happened
in 1896, and since then we've sat
in that cavernous movie dark, heads
lifted to the screen to watch tutorials

on how to do it—how much lip, tongue,
which way to tilt our heads—to the right,
one researcher's found, at least 65% of us.
50% of us have our first kiss before

fourteen, and the average woman kisses
seventy-nine men before she marries.
Between that first kiss and the kiss
for Mr. Eighty, millions of bacteria

will emigrate from mouth to mouth,
bringing us the prospect of cavities,
colds or the flu, a bit of yesterday's lunch.
But when I found my Mr. Eighty,

all I wanted to do was lean in with eyes closed,
kiss and kiss this one man promising me
the infinite, our faith indivisible, incalculable
pleasure from his lips to mine, whatever it cost.

—*Allison Joseph*

On a Record James Agee Recites from Memory His Poems, Auden's, Shakespeare's, Etc.

Here is where it hits me in the heart—
The Lord's Prayer. I have said it, in bed,
forever, twenty thousand times. I have heard
close-cropped Episcopalians, tall in suits
behind me say the words, some theatrically,
some to hide with the voice-wind around us.

But to hear him pray it, his voice less boisterous
and Southern than I'd expected, that "gain"
in "against us" more British, is to come too close,
to wedge beneath his breath, to touch, be touched
too deep: a kiss in the ear, a whisper of God's home
number. I shouldn't think this way about a dead man,
a married one at that, but dead is not a word for him.

Not while letters form words.

—Tina Kelley

In That Instant

Just there...in a lapse that time shifts through...I remember
my yellow scarf, your gold earring, the way clouds dragged
their shadows into the river—sky and water. (Blue. White.
Gray.) That day we climbed the side of a covered bridge,
onto the roof—the pitch hard-angled, dangerously steep.
Narrow planks lifted and dipped where we stepped—so
easy to be that reckless, that young. When you pulled me
close at the top and kissed me, someone below yelled *jump*.
In that instant, I almost thought we might.

—*Adele Kenny*

Kissed

Last night I was kissed. Twice.
Not passionate kisses. Don't think
Rodin's lovers, the man's colossal hand spliced

to her slender thigh, her bare arm linked
to his neck, bringing his mouth to hers,
that kind of romantic lip-sync.

And please don't imagine what occurs
when Europeans meet: kissing the right cheek
then the left, however many times one prefers.

But kisses, affectionate and genuine, neither meek
nor expected: first a man then
a woman. To his credit, he did speak

first, saying *it's good to see you* when
we joined him and his friend at the restaurant.
May I kiss you? he asked, knowing I'd been

grieving. Also sensing I'd want
to be asked. In sum, a gallant gay man
unafraid of being tender. I'm no savant

but my woman friend had no game plan
to bestow a kiss on my cheek as we said good night,
but kiss me she did. Two in one night's span:

two not to be dismissed, two friends right
in their instinct that a touch, a kiss
was just what I needed and more than polite.

—*Claire Keyes*

Kissing

Everyone likes it, right? Mafiosi, grandmas, lovers.
Especially lovers. Which brings us to the question,
        did Joseph ever kiss Mary? In the Uffizi, you look
at pictures of Mary and Joseph and wonder if he
        ever tried to, well, you know. Okay, not that, but didn't
he at least try to kiss her? In Gentile da Fabriano's
        painting, Joseph looks too tired to nod to the magi

as they arrive with their knickknacks, much less
offer them a seat, cup of wine, piece of pita bread,
        whereas Lorenzo Monaco's Joseph is fit, alert, and not
old at all or at least no older than I, whose days
        of producing a photo ID in order to buy a downmarket
beer or rum collins are behind him by decades yet
        who is as fond of kissing as ever—fonder, really.

What happens in our brains when we kiss? Scientists
say our brains create a chemical cocktail consisting
        of dopamine, oxytocin, and serotonin. Dopamine
stimulates the same area of the brain activated by
        heroin and cocaine, resulting in euphoria and addictive
behavior, whereas oxytocin, which is released during
        childbirth and breastfeeding, fosters feelings of affection

and attachment, and serotonin reaches levels in the brain
when people kiss that look a lot like those of someone
        with obsessive compulsive disorder, which is why
the brain scan of a person who's just sitting there
        minding his or her business looks like a satellite image

of North Korea at night whereas a scan of the brain
        of that same person kissing looks like Times Square

        on New Year's Eve. No wonder the memory of
a good kiss can stay with us for years. I mean,
        we can't say what love is anyway. Raymond Carver
says, "It ought to make us feel ashamed when we talk
        like we know what we're talking about when we talk
about love." But a kiss? That's something else.
        That right there is a whole different ball game,

        shooting match, kettle of fish. That's the kind of thing
that gets folks sexed up. It's like when Dante sees
        Beatrice and says, "Here is a god stronger than I
who is coming to rule over me," even though he never
        kisses her at all, and Catherine Earnshaw in *Wuthering
Heights* to say of Edgar Linton, "I love the ground
        under his feet, and the air over his head, and everything

        he touches and every word he says. I love all his looks,
and all his actions and him entirely and all together,"
        even though it turns out that her true love is Heathcliff.
Oh, coulda woulda shoulda. Love is love and not fade away,
        says Buddy Holly, also the Rolling Stones. Of course
Joseph kissed Mary. And she kisses him back. Don't they
        look happy? And then Jesus is born. It's a miracle.

—*David Kirby*

Sweetgrass

In the crushing heat of a summer afternoon,
we lay by the pond, chewing sweetgrass,
dreaming our lives into the future

where the boys we loved would be men
and we loving wives and mothers. We knew
nothing about women's imprisonment

in marriages where their lives disappeared
like stains in the wash or crumbs from the table.
We had no idea of the struggle ahead.

Bumblebees sank to the clover, Old Bill
in the barn above nuzzled hay and snuffled,
shaking off flies. We chewed and whispered

the names of coveted boys, feeling our bodies
flutter where we weren't used to feeling them
flutter. From there, not long to the afternoon

in the loft of the hay barn while Old Bill stood
sleeping below us and we pretended to be
the boy the other loved, my turn, then hers,

kissing and kissing, illicit, delicious,
each thinking the flutter a secret, dreaming
all we'd do to make it come again.

—*Lynne Knight*

The Kissing Disease

Isn't that what they called it? The fever
you could catch from pressing your lips
to the lips of another in the dark corner
of the gym after the game, or later,
lying down in the rough bramble
of the field. Wasn't that how it began?
And didn't it lead to a long malaise—
a month in bed, swollen glands
of the neck? You had to sip hot fluids,
eat crackers laced with salt, lie down
until it passed. What a way to meet
the god of want, slack deity who slips
into the back of your throat, microscopic
germ. The way we learn desire
is a contagion cast from one body
to the next. Something you contract
by getting close enough to inhale
the whiff of musk rising from her
like a lick of flame. Or from feeling
his shirt shake beneath your palm—
the dizzy of his heart. Bitter particle,
trick spore. Microbe hidden
in the volcano of the mouth.
Malady of the young, virus
of the tonsil, the tongue. What
can we say of how it enters the blood,
scorches a path through the veins,
sickens us with hunger, shapes
the course of what's to come.

—*Danusha Laméris*

To Alchemy

Salt crystals turning into sea monkeys, salamanders
into witches, a sip of wine into the jeweled
blood of God. I've always loved your presto
change-o miracles. Here I am, middle-aged
and mortgaged, and still I believe.
Sitting down to play Brahms, I hope
to be converted into electric mist
or a flock of wrens. When my father died,
I went bowling—anything to transform
the avalanche behind my breastbone
into crashes I could hear. After my third game,
I tossed down fifty dollars and walked
away wearing grief size twelve and a half,
grief in shades of smoke and blood
I could lace myself. We need you, Alchemy,
because darkness beckons, because the body
bruises easily, can't fly or burrow,
can never find the ignition in the time machine.
Some evenings all I want to do is dial
the dead, or redecorate my garden
using falling stars and the cat in my lap.
Just once let me take a bath
in fire, then hatch anew from my ashes.
Just once let me be a sophomore again.
Make it the Friday before Christmas,
me beside the Coke machine
in the school gym holding mistletoe
above my head: waiting for nirvana to walk by
in a drill team sweater and ghostly
perfume, and convert my blind mouth into a kiss.

—*Lance Larsen*

Kissing

They are kissing, on a park bench,
on the edge of an old bed, in a doorway
or on the floor of a church. Kissing
as the streets fill with balloons
or soldiers, locusts or confetti, water
or fire or dust. Kissing down through
the centuries under sun or stars, a dead tree,
an umbrella, amid derelicts. Kissing
as Christ carries his cross, as Gandhi
sings his speeches, as a bullet
careens through the air toward a child's
good heart. They are kissing,
long, deep, spacious kisses, exploring
the silence of the tongue, the mute
rungs of the upper palate, hungry
for the living flesh. They are still
kissing when the cars crash and the bombs
drop, when the babies are born crying
into the white air, when Mozart bends
to his bowl of soup and Stalin
bends to his garden. They are kissing
to begin the world again. Nothing
can stop them. They kiss until their lips
swell, their thick tongues quickening
to the budded touch, licking up
the sweet juices. I want to believe
they are kissing to save the world,
but they're not. All they know
is this press and need, these two-legged

beasts, their faces like roses crushed
together and opening, they are covering
their teeth, they are doing what they have to do
to survive the worst, they are sealing
the hard words in, they are dying
for our sins. In a broken world they are
practicing this simple and singular act
to perfection. They are holding
onto each other. They are kissing.

                        —*Dorianne Laux*

Learning to Paint

Eagle Creek Trailer Court, 1968

It was the time we found all those cans in an empty house and transformed a stranger's floor into a work of art. We pried open gallons of bathroom pink and kitchen green, swirled patterns with curtain rods plucked from the windows, skied across wet canvas. We tossed our shoes in someone else's trash, sneaked through our own back door.

We ran a hot bath, climbed in both at once—shoved our paint-laden clothes in the washer. Scrubbing until our skin reddened, we lay back at either end of the tub, the toes of one even with the ears of the other, and began to talk about boys.

Lying there in hot water with the washer agitating we wondered aloud how our first kiss might be. Lisa said we had to be ready or no one would ever kiss us. She said *like this* and I watched her lips pooch out and smack the soft skin of her hand just above the crease of thumb. *Sit up. Pretend you're a boy.*

The air was steamy. I did what Lisa said. Water sloshed over the edge and when I leaned to blot it she kissed me. She tipped her head and said *now you kiss me* and I did. *Again,* she said and we did, our lips learning to be ready.

We kissed there in the bathtub until the washing machine shuddered to a stop and we began to shiver. Lisa pulled the drain plug. We sat hugging our knees, watching water sluice past our haunches and through the arches of our feet.

—*Jenifer Browne Lawrence*

Eve and Lilith Go to Macy's

In the fitting room at Macy's
Eve shimmies into a pair of leopard-print leggings
then mocks a dance pose.
"OMG! You're hotter than a habanero in those pants,"
gasps Lilith. She slides her finger
down Eve's shapely hip
as though striking a match
then blows out her finger.

Eve can't believe how good that feels
through the cotton-polyester-spandex blend.
Lilith always went for men in a big way
but maybe the oversexed act
was overcompensation, a put-on.
Maybe Lilith is gay.
Maybe *I'm* gay, thinks Eve
wishing her friend would touch her again.

In the Macy's fitting room
with the triple-paneled mirror
the women's figures mingle and multiply.
Looking at one of her selves
Eve moves her right arm
but in the mirror it looks like her left arm.
She can't be sure which image
reflects the real Eve.

In the champagne of the moment
she turns to Lilith, the real one, the warm one

intending to bestow upon her
an air kiss of gratitude
at most a smooch on the cheek

but Lilith catches Eve's mouth,
draws her to her other self.
Eve can't remember
when she's ever had a kiss like that.
Maybe she never has, never will again
so what is the point in stopping?

The women linger in each other's arms
as the hidden security camera
looks on with its mysterious eye.
And the women are okay with that.
They know that eye sees all things.
Sees all. Says nothing.

—Lynn Levin

He Delivers Unto Her His Kisses

There is much to celebrate. She invites moments of unaccountable happiness. They hide from the photographers. The cook invents traditional dishes, invites her into the kitchen and whispers the legend of his origins while, for luck, he traces her own history from lips to waist with his good hand, her profile shuddering under his measure, his mouth a recipe for kissing. The guests prepare for after-dinner struggles with lubricious budding beaus. The entire nation awaits the birth of the beauty, the exotic, the blessed.

Stay, my treasure.

She can do anything she wants with him. Her flattery is nothing because he is already convinced. She is laughing with her contessa's voice; everyone admires the perfect red of her lines, sultry sway of her lines while the orchestra plays mazurkas, the men compare their stripes and ribbons. She trembles beneath her own little uniform, mismatched and tattered. There would be fanfares, antiphonal and filled with brass.

He promises her a little farm in the south with olive trees and amber light. Still, the night manager, a colonel, threatens to throw them out on the street for the indecency of their love. The colonel sees himself in bed clutching her, growing hot with the metallic clank of his medals. She lifts the colonel's palm to the offending place, but keeps the tone of her voice serious and complicitous, gives him half-smiles and adds some new detail or other each time she assures him it will not happen again.

She remembers what Kundera said about love, that it does not make itself felt in the desire for sex (a desire, he wrote, that extends to the universe of women) but in the desire for shared sleep (a desire limited to her). Kundera, after all, wrote about her niece. Her lover says that kissing her with the tip of the tongue feels like ice cream melting. Her lover says she has taught him that certain sounds have a soul. Her lover says that their touching comprises the place where their many sounds merge into a soul.

She has brought along five changes of clothes, and with each change she is more herself. Kisses, he tells her, are miracles the flesh tries to duplicate. He offers up his own strangeness. They are building each other a shelter in the larger spaces of their bodies, where they step out of time.

He blesses her. The air smells of damp earth, of spilled chocolate, and from time to time, she recognizes some land brought back by gusts of wind. With faith she delves into the customs of the world stirring below and when she feels hungry, she eats. And why not? It is all her doing, and he kisses her again.

—*Jeffrey Levine*

Forgetting She's Dead I Dream Adrienne Rich

vital and limber and overflowing the stage
with words set to music and words bright on film
and her face a moon and an owl and a fox
as hundreds of young people and thousands of old
transform with her eyes and her voice and her body
into colors that join and swirl and rise
to make the gray world change from frozen bones
into the dance her bold life believed
courageous art can inspire and lead
and then she's reaching for my worn hand
and pulling me onto the shining boards
and kissing my face wet with new tears
and everywhere flowers hot crimson wide roses
keep opening as in each other's arms
we fill the theater with the light of her poems

—*Katharyn Howd Machan*

Skin Rising

You say the bites are kisses,
that they swell
toward heaven white,
red about the edges, sucked by
angels, their mosquito hisses
hesitating like his brother wishing
Abel wasn't right. This other hell
inside the veins transmitted
from one to one to one: the perfect legend
of blood, betrayal, suffering, and kisses.
We swat at such divinity; we itch
for it, the summer filled with misses
and mistakes. Behind the hedge
it's Cain alone who yells;
the angels bite his heels and his legs
then flap and flip into his eyes and nose.
The clicking wings that suck our sin and go
into another teach us how to sip
what starts out sweet, diffuses into dull.
These are angels whispering in my head,
the after-echo of the morning bells;

they tell me bites are kisses
that they swell into the mouth
and loiter in the lungs; the heavy wishes
settle in the liver, but the rest
become the face and soul, become the glistening
within the eyes. Now insect-like

we flit and lick and see about all sides,
our feet still sticky on each other's skin.
The wings are light and veil us from sin
that bites our kisses, kisses all our bites.

—*Marjorie Maddox*

Paris, 1936

after a photo by Brassaï

The couple in the carnival swan boat doesn't see
the camera, which has captured them, mid-kiss,
at the height of their aerial arc.
They are young, at home in this fragile gondola,
with its hull, thin as a Sèvres finger bowl and dented
at the prow, with its looping neck and staring,
painted eyes. She leans back in the stern,
smiling, her own eyes closed, her lips open
to his like the borders of a friendly nation.
Standing, he bends down to her, easy as Charon
in his tight shirt and natty trousers, his hand
resting lightly on the carriage pole.
Behind them, the sky is clear and the sun
stains the ground with spreading shadows,
and somewhere, you can be sure,
an old man is calling, *Look out!—it's reckless to fly,
backward and standing, in a gilded teacup!*
but they are deaf to warnings, fixed,
in the high, interminable instant of the kiss,
weightless, before the blind rush to earth.

—*Jennifer Maier*

A Blessing Via Skype

for Ravi, nearly a year and a half

I see you!—we speak and wave
play peek-a-boo with upside-down plastic
yellow-gold dinner plate—uneaten
stuffing forms sticky spirals in downy
light brown hair   Let's take inventory
mimic each other—yes
lift strands of hair—pat nose—
bare lips to show teeth—locate
ears—imagine, one on each side of our heads!
I blow him kisses and he
blows kisses back from the palm
of chubby wide-open fingers
Oh, I say, *I hug you, luscious baby*
my arms hug pretend he's inside them
and he wraps arms around himself
virtual hug in turn and *Oh*
Oh, I kiss you, Ravi, and he
leans forward to kiss my face
on the tablet! *He's never done*
that before! says Daddy,
my grandson.
            And I rise brimful
of warm milky way stars radiant
meteor bubbles swirling in space
underwater gemstone grottoes
aquamarine blue cobalt sun-loving coral
undulating seagrasses to glow
throughout and beyond my life

towards a next world
his great-grandpa and I
carrying Ravi's computer screen kiss—
infinities in the palm of my hand—
through a color-spangled cosmos.

—*Charlotte Mandel*

Strawberries, Limoncello, Water Ice, Passing Time

You bring home Italian Market strawberries
so ripe they'll be ruined if we don't eat them today

so after dinner I wash, core and halve them
as you water plants off the deck, the last of the sunlight

purpling the sky. I drop the strawberries
into a bowl over lemon water ice,

add a shot of *limoncello* from a bottle given us
last Christmas, carry the bowl and two spoons

up to our bedroom, trying not to dig in
before you join me for a movie. But I can't;

it's too good, so sugary, so cold, while the day's been
so hot we ate dinner without shirts. I can taste

fresh lemon peel in the homemade *limoncello*
as if Christmas were yesterday, not half a year ago.

I pluck a strawberry from the bowl and study it close
as the water shuts off and you curl away the hose—

such scarlet skin, so many tiny seeds, every one
a wonder. My fingers redden with juice,

grow sticky-sweet with water ice. When you come in
I pop the strawberry in my mouth, a guilty child,

thinking of a sunburn long ago,
how you rubbed my skin aloe-cool, and then

rubbed me again, stirring blood, ripening stamen
until I seeded red skin and took safety in

the false comfort there would be time enough
for everything. Our bed creaks as you crawl in.

You fluff your pillow; I spoon you water ice and
a strawberry half, its white V within—this moment

a victory. A drip hits my chest and you kiss it away.
What flavor is inside our selves?

Sweetness, surely, the way you lap at my heart—
like strawberries, *limoncello*, water ice, passing time.

—*Kelly McQuain*

To Church, To Market

Who couldn't fall in love
over nectarines

two chins cupping juice
the confluence between

jaw/jaw peach/plum his/her
palm atop palm.

Here in the market, stand
how many ways to kiss

over corn, make church
in the hollow of strawberry.

Find yourself with the young
dahlia grower and find yourself

behind tent. Himalayan berry
in reach. Thorns may seek

your hands, offer them
as you would before Easter.

For now, there is river
enough for cleansing.

Whiskey, like summer
in your teacup.

—*Natasha Moni*

May Day Kiss

May arrives in buzz and blossom.
Come my love, listen to the bumblebees
in the locust tree, their hum swallowed
under a conundrum of white petals.
Look how these laden branches arch
over the aching green of the yard.
Inhale their honey scent that lures
our heavy-winged hearts to the flower's core,
then up into the shocking blue petticoat of this sky
recently stripped of its tedious gray skirt.
I bury my wrinkled face into the curve of your neck.
Let May harbor our unwelcome pain.
My lips open to drink this air, to savor
the salty shore of your skin.
My tongue quivers like a fin, eager
to swim again into your slippery pink mouth.

—*Ruth Mota*

Down Time

I read on the internet that the fish oil
my cardio prescribed may also shake
away the blues that sway my moods,
which makes me wonder if the good
will of fish is contagious. So I've
earth-googled my development to see
if a neighbor has a pond where a school
of cheerful koi swish their feathery tails
back and forth, back and forth, the way
my wife and I once swished back and forth
before she left me for a better dancer.
I have to tell you, I'm not pleased that koi
can live longer than people, especially me.
Me and my chubby heart beating back
and forth, struggling to keep up, causing
my chest to throb, which is why the doc
also prescribed tiny nitro pills should
that fish swimming in the small ocean
of my chest get tired of flapping its fins.
I rise out of my recliner, go outside,
stroll past the mortgaged houses and turn
into the yard of a foreclosed neighbor
who couldn't keep it up. I walk by
his wilted hydrangea, his exhausted hyacinths,
his pooped belladonna and find the murky pool
where the *Cyprinus carpio*, fat with Omega-3,
are floating on their backs. Their once
carroty skins are now the color of Kansas.
I want to pump their little chests,

kiss their slippery lips, bring them back
to life so they can make me happy.
Instead, I turn from their fishy graveyard
and trudge home to a cup of chamomile tea
offered by my wife who returned to me
when she got tired of dancing. She asks
if I had a good walk as she hands me
two gelatin globules the color of koi.
I thank my lucky days, my lucky nights.
I thank my lucky stars, my one lucky moon,
my beautiful wife. I kiss her lips. I catch
my breath. I sit down to rest. I sip my tea.
I take my meds.

—*Peter E. Murphy*

Birdman

Every morning, my Amazon parrot greets me
as he has since the day I bought him
for ten bucks on a dusty road
with his downcast rage and broken wing.

Hello Birdman, I say, and from his iron cage
he chirps like a telephone, lowers his yellow head,
so I can scratch the down beneath his pin feathers,
lift him to my lips for a clucky kiss.

For over four decades, he's hated
first my boyfriends, then my husbands, three dogs, and a cat.
On the October morning when I carried my swaddled
twins into the sunroom and set them in the bassinet,
he watched with one yellow eye, tilted his head,
raked the air with his screams. Oh, he's full of loathing,
my little green man.

How could he have known—as he flew
above the *milpas* in Hermosillo, before some kid
shot off his wing—that for the rest of his life,
he would live with a giant companion looming
over him with heavy bones and fleshy claws.

And how could I have known my prince
would fill a space in the chaos
three inches wide and eight inches long, that he would
kiss me at dawn with his Bakelite beak and
dry tongue— wear a plumed suit the color of lawn.

—Dion O'Reilly

Concealed Carry

How is a gun like a kiss?
We held each other after the love-making—sheets tender as wounds.
Was the gun solid in my hand? Was it a tiffany blue?
I woke in the rain-gnawed way of a cold four a.m. to gunfire out on
            Rockbridge Road: five blasts, close-on. Voices yelling.
My pulse raced as they sounded, but I turned over, face-down
            into the mouthy darkness—tried to sleep again.
We'd taken our time for each other: the desire building. I'd listened
            to his drawl on the phone
                for over half a year: asking for my patience. It had been
                too cold, a worker's transmission had gone out. I watched
                his forearms, once my house was almost rebuilt. I looked
                at his hands: the wedding band gone.
I moved back in, & he came to do unexpected jobs: painting
            baseboards, hanging pictures.
We had little in common, and I didn't imagine a man who hunted,
            a man who kept a gun in his truck—a man who drove a
            truck—for god's sake—could be so damn good at kissing.
Because that's all we did for two months after I said to him—
            now, I'm going to kiss you. So we took our time.
When he said *have you ever been to that pawn shop?* I wondered
            if he'd been there before. He
                knew my color: that exact shade of blue—
I didn't like the weighty danger in my palm. No matter how
            good it looked. Bullets, I reasoned, couldn't save me
            from a future I'd never know.
He wasn't a man who trusted easily, but sometimes it was a solid
            hour of our mouths on
                each other—he teased me to no end. His tongue

finding everything about me. We were raw in the
everyday light of dawn, but that only meant I knew
him for his hurt, & he knew me for mine.
It's easy to cave in to kisses & guns—to say that what I want is
what I need.
That morning on Rockbridge, the repo man was shot by the car's
owner, who then shot himself in the foot. Everyone—
luckily—still alive.
But that's what I'm saying—the accuracy is just not there: bullets
or kisses. Kisses: how they multiplied up and down my neck
with his low growl. Kisses: wounding when they disappear.
We risked each other in the unstarred midnight—our mouths
wordless—a wilderness of presence, need, where we found
each other lost, then entered each other again.

—*Amy Pence*

Written Kisses

The X's I sometimes make
below my signed name
are shorthand for the birds
artists at one time placed
around a love god's head.

Songbirds. Small. In flight.
Wings spread, bodies straight.
A chorus circling Eros. Singers
that people began to portray
as two bold pen-strokes.

A line from upper left
to bottom right, another
to cross it from high to low,
and I've set love
loose into the page's sky.

Thin black birds sing
the tunes learned as they flew
circles around the divine.
From under my name,
their inky voices rise.

—*Paulann Petersen*

Crush, Texas

*William George Crush conceived of a train wreck as a
spectacle. No admission was charged, and train fares to the
crash site were sold for $2 from any location in Texas. About
40,000 people showed up on September 15, 1896, making
the new town of Crush, Texas, temporarily the second-largest
city in the state.*

Why don't you put on that antique swallow necklace
before you dress and come downstairs for breakfast?
The one I got in Spain. Not quite precious
metal, but the Deco style curves the edges
and softens patinaed bronze and the swallows' restless
flight on delicate porcelain, the nexus
of breasts, our hearts, our corresponding sexes.

The thought of that pendant makes my hands nearly reckless
for balance, to become the ambidextrous
beloved who loves to lose at Os and Xs.
Our children sleep. Come down. Come here. Perplex us
with swallows, voracious with your reflexes,
with the crush of you in the terrible state of Texas
that like a staged train wreck (in a good way) wrecks us.

—*John Poch*

First Kiss

With Cindy's divorced Mom mysteriously absent,
we spun the bottle in her basement
to the voices of Blood, Sweat and Tears,
Neil Young aching from the HiFi.
When the bare snout of the seagreen bottle pointed
at Jim Burbach, he didn't pause, he pulled me up
off the shag carpet and led me into the playroom
whose paneless doors and windows kept us within
reach of all my friends,
though I had no fear,
figuring a kiss was a simple
matching of sorts, like one sock laid atop another
in a scented drawer,
lips pressed to lips creating
a unified whole, a sealed body of trust,
not this tongue--slick and more certain
than I'd ever been of anything,
darting its way through my mouth like a serpent
coiling through a gash in my life
as if this were its true beginning.

—*Andrea Potos*

That Startled Space

Caught under a yard-high waterfall
in the narrow river,
a child's red rubber ball
and an empty water bottle tumble,
and thoughts return, son,

how you left without my having felt
your final warmth—
a life kept inside me,
safe in womb water

until it was time to separate—
you to breathe on your own.
You scored a perfect 10
on the Apgar scale.

Pool water your last inhale,
lungs filled, body cooled to cold
and blue rigidity as you sank
into another kind of water world—
only I wasn't there.

I wasn't there the next morning
when they found you on the bottom
and brought you out—the mouth
I never kissed goodbye,
covered in bloody froth—

I now left, as Rilke wrote,
... in the startled space
which a youth as lovely as a god
had suddenly left forever ...

Over and over, again and again
the ball and bottle circle, tossed
against the curtain of water, trapped
in foam, the ongoing turmoil.

                              —*Wanda S. Praisner*

Five Thousand Times

If it's true—you, me,
five thousand times

more likely to crash in a car
than in a plane—we should kiss

as we are kissing now—outside
the airport, in this downpour—

every bleary morning, every time
one of us grabs the keys,

kiss hard enough to register
the friction, the precise

tilt of our heads, hint of salt
on our lips, heat or thaw

of something nebulous,
edgeless, a thing we long

to carry—the sway of all
our many-weathered kisses,

fringe of every held breath,
and this one-and-only gaze

in the rain, in the splatter,
the car horns and thunder—

one of us to head inside,
the other to drive away,

our last smiles flashing
through the pulse of wipers—

fast, faster—sweeping blades.

—*Christine Rhein*

Encyclopedia of Kisses

The kind that graffiti themselves into your girlhood, work like flashlights
illuminating the end of Chemistry. Kisses like strands of the double helix

or the crocus on the way home that you have never understood before.
Kisses from Raul, from Henri, though not dreamt of at the same time.

You heard rumors of the crossed boundaries of tongue and hard-
edge of teeth that could open like suitcases. Had plans for a tin of lip balm.

Later, inside the movie theater, in the middle of *Night of the Living Dead*—
goodbye to girlhood, to horseback riding. The whole palaver of violins

and roses means nothing when compared to popcorn kisses
in the almost dark. This exchange of dangerous lips with Richard Maxfield

meant endless love, meant nearly marriage; after all, we had kissed—
explored the ridgelines at the top of each other's mouths,

inhaled *M&M* breath. This—meant—something.
In the morning the world appeared different, the oatmeal sweeter.

Each spot where our lips had touched held a new atom
of pleasure, a science experiment held in abeyance.

—*Susan Rich*

Watching You, Father, Almost Thanksgiving, St. Mary's ICU

What's this? you ask of your mother's
ruby signet ring on my finger. *Pretty,*
you say, pulling my hand toward your lips—

fading to sleep before you might kiss...
Can't rouse, can't leave you—
I sit, nibbling on my nails

bitter from your disinfectant.
Sixty sweeps of the red clock hand,
overhead vents throbbing

from a distant generator.
This is how it's been—watching you
in the sleep of your life.

Your hands clutch and unclutch.
Fingers thrum and wag.
Cell memories will

your ninety-year-old body
to dance what you didn't dance;
to shadow box causes not squared;

to slip, again, this Lippóczy family ring
from your finger onto mine,
graduation day, Windows on the World.

I raise my fist to press, press my lips
into this blood stone that once emblazoned
wild birds into hot wax, ancient letters.

—*Susanna Rich*

Many Rivers

You kissed the sole
of my foot this morning
before you left for work, and the back
of my thigh, and my right
hip. I know millions of kisses
have been given and received—
I know they have fallen out of the sky
like snow onto my foremothers,
so many bodies touched
by so many lips,
all the songs of skin and breath perhaps
already sung. But I also know
there are fewer thorns in my feet now,
I have waded many rivers to get here,
and if I lie down in this clearing
while the rain creeps across the hillsides
it is only because you have given me
what I didn't know to ask for.

—*Katherine Riegel*

Kissing

Any kisses from the first five years are forgotten.
And the ones from relatives, forgettable.
Many kisses from my mother; none from my father.
And that first other one
from Bonnie
under a dining room table at a birthday party.
Her chocolate tongue was sweet,
but we were hiding, embarrassed.
Kissing was something we weren't supposed to do.
But it wasn't the attraction of the forbidden
that put our lips together
and when tongues met
it just seemed right.
Then, we felt some shame
and as the birthday girl opened her presents,
we didn't look at each other,
as if we had opened some gift
that was not ours to open.

—Kenneth Ronkowitz

Cause and Effect

after Dean Young

Because we are so thoughtless
we kiss each other on the holes

we speak from, we cross our legs
upon each other, angling in,

always angling in. The fireplace
is electric, but that doesn't stop

our melding on the hardwood.
Because we are so hungry we stare

like owls at the bar-lit faces
of strangers we know

we're supposed to want.
You are a deep-sea diver

and I'm an inactive volcano.
You are a starfish and I'm

a rash from a wetsuit. You are
four honeymooners and I'm

the blonde walking by.
Because we are so close

our fingertips catch. You plunge us
into the ocean. I speak in bubbles.

You grow a shell and I'm the grit
in your mantle. We irritate

each other. We produce a pearl.

—*Dan Rosenberg*

First Seating

Flu season, so we're not kissing
unless you count the smooches we wave
to each other as we sit down to eat.
We'll be out before the second seating
comes in with glitter eyes and muscled arms
that reach across the table to hold hands
and order tapas to share as they dip their forks
from one dish to the other, from one mouth
to the other, their evening beginning
as I tuck myself into bed, flossed and moisturized.
By the time they've paid their bill,
I'll have embarked on my tossed journey,
flanneled in a bed that knows
the contours of my body as well as I do.
I should begrudge them their passion,
but I've my own circadian rhythm that knows
the leftovers I brought home may not be as full
of promise as lithe tongues dancing together,
but I've eaten this meal once already,
and I know it will be good tomorrow.

—*Susan Rothbard*

Marriage in June

And here we are, a little drunk at noon,
eyes closed, holding hands on the porch
as if on a ship in the Caribbean,

my glass of Riesling tilting, your breath
heavy, thick in the heat as you doze,
our lawn overgrowing itself,
lush and ignored, reaching for clouds.

I smell the sun in your hair, hot, citrusy,
a bit of sweat lifting from your skin (or is it mine?),
and the mealy bite of overturned soil from where
we planted tomatoes this morning,

and I wish I could stay here forever,
tasting the salt on my lips,
that kiss in the dirt and work.

We could live on those tomatoes
and the Myer lemons from the small tree

we planted last summer, on a day
like today, when we bought a shovel, dug,
our fingers touching in soil,
flirting in the wet earth,

the heat a hazy shimmer, dropping us
to the grass, dreaming of fruit.

—*Leigh Camacho Rourks*

Confessions

1.

If you kiss
My neck and squeeze
My hips at the same time
I will melt into you.
I will do anything you
Want me to, I'll moan
Your name all night long,
And in the morning
I promise I'll put on a
Respectable dress
And go to church
With your mother.

2.

I had a vision
Where you kissed
The back of my neck,
And ran the tip of your tongue
Down my spine
And now I have to speak to
Someone else
About something else and
Stop myself
From moaning out
loud.

—*Rajwant Saghera*

Alone Together in Church

This must be in the present
tense, because it's the blue
moment I live in forever.

This must be in the present
tense, because our theology
says we go on changed utterly

but still ourselves, the one thing
I cling to because we are atoms
of each other, we are defined

by each other eternally and nothing
has happened to change that.
This solitude together is after

all have gone from the wake.
After the fickle friends and the genuine
strangers have gone, after

the priest has left, letting me
lock up later, I alone remain
with you, attentive in vigil.

How solitude magnifies.
I look around the stillness for us,
the empty nave in which I hold

your still-warm folded hands.
The Altar's flickering votive lamp
casts its garnet prism over the magnificence

of your patriarchal beard in state.
Father, because you are transfigured,
I am transfigured against my will.

Because it is so quiet, I hold you
in focused belief. Flesh and spirit.
Because we are father and son before God,

and this is our present forever,
I continue us sleeping and awake. I lean
into you and kiss the communion of your lips.

—*Nicholas Samaras*

Unmarked

for Natalie

So much like sequins
the sunlight on this river.
Something like that kiss—

remember?
Fourth of July, with the moon
down early   the air moved

as if it were thinking,
as if it had begun
to understand

how hard it is
to feel at home
in the world,

but that night
she found a place
just above your shoulder

and pressed her lips
there. Soft rain

had called off the fireworks:
the sky was quiet, but
back on Earth

two boys cruised by on bikes
trying out bad words. You turned
to reach her mouth,

at last, with yours   after weeks
of long walks, talking

about former loves
gone awry—

how the soul finally
falls down

and gets up alone
once more

finding the city strange,
the streets unmarked.

Every time you meet someone
it's hard not to wonder

who they've been—one story
breaking so much

into the next: memory
engraves its hesitations—

but that night
you found yourself
unafraid. Do you remember

what the wind told the trees
about her brown hair?—
how the cool dark turned around:

that first kiss,
long as a river.

Didn't it seem like you already loved her?

Off the sidewalk: a small pond,
the tall cattails, all those sleepy koi

coloring the water.

—Tim Seibles

Looking into Milano

They have the lowest birth rate in Europe, but
Italians are, yes, skilled in sensuality—foods, fabrics,
frescoes, bronzes, marbles, oils, foreplay.

                                        I had left behind
those icy clerks in Bern (never saw a couple holding hands,
never a single peck on a Swiss cheek). On the Alpine downslope
into Milano palm trees rustled, caressed . . . Metro, then out
into a vast piazza:

                    GLORY. Pigeons shit their welcome
onto my suitcase. *Glory,* yes, though facing the duomo a long
city block of garish ads (aspirin to underwear to wine and watches)
—but still, that fantasy cathedral, smack on the site
of the Roman basilica. I drew sketches, took photos.

                                        When did I notice
the couple on the bench? That neither had leaned away even to gaze
into the other's eyes, had not separated lips in half an hour? A gentle
circling, barely bussing, as if conscientiously spreading her lipstick
evenly . . . I circumnavigated the building that took seven centuries
to complete. The Candoglia marble is arranged Gothic-ish,

                                                more like
Disney than Renaissance. And so was the couple, still at it, lips lightly
touching, lightly (not exactly what I would call kissing) when I cut
through the Galleria to La Scala where the fashionable loitered
haughtily, a dozen or so Carabinieri scanning the crowd,

                                                peering
down side streets in their killer Armani uniforms, strapped operatically
to black machine guns. I strode across town. Leonardo's famous
failure, desperate eggshells of color clinging to a mainly blank wall,
Michelangelo's unfinished *Pietà,*

attenuated, hacked, nursing home
futility slashed all over it. Un panino al tonno, café doppio, and I limped
back into Piazza del Duomo to see *them*, my God, still at it! Could it be
the same couple? I checked my notes: same shiny brown hair, black
stilettos, leather coats, jade earrings, his light gray wools with the stain
at the crotch.

 I looked for a camera crew, but this was no shoot, no
stunt. Were they robots? Never an auditory smooch. Ethereal, super-
natural. My testicles ached for them. I have seen cinematic kisses
all over Italy, but why this marathon and right out in the open?
There was no tension or the slightest sign of strain.

 Was it a
game? More Brancusi than Rodin, they were level, neither bent back
like the helpless, swooning sailor's girl in Times Square or like
Canova's Psyche looped in Cupid's reviving arms. Equality. Mutual
tactile attention raised to the level of prayer. *Devotion*, I whispered.
Good Catholics, let's say, they could wait for a wedding night.
Meantime, chapped lips, blue balls, cramps, and spasms.

 Four hours.
I wore a stopwatch in those days and timed my walks, had seen
a Verona sidewalk festive with used condoms. I longed
to interview them. But they never opened their eyes. Maybe they
were blind?

 To this day I remember that swirling not-quite-kiss
better than the gold Madonnina on the duomo's highest spire, better
than the navigli from the quarries of Lago Maggiore.

 As well as I
remember Ambrose's shocking corpse, a little skin and hair clinging
to his skull. Noseless, all dressed up in gold and jewels, silks and satins,
waiting for Judgment Day. Milano, yes, I saw it all with my own
lonely, secular eyes.

—*Ron Smith*

First Bases

If Mae West was right—a man's kiss
is his signature—then sign on again
across the faded ink of the first fool
to fall for my smile, the haunted-house

smooch starting in a rickety car, Scott's
hand snaking up my shirt, my lips
parting after a peck. Let's mimic Rodin's
lovers in *The Kiss;* I'll throw my arm

over your neck, your hand at my waist.
Morning won't send this again: child
asleep, quiet house holding its breath
against cold autumn winds. I was two

years old when I first pursed and closed
my eyes, a neighbor's house framing
the photo of my lips pressed to a red
tulip. When I hold stems again, a bundle

of nodding bells, I recall the soft palm
of a hand that drew me in for a kiss
collapsed—he a former student. I should've
let our lips brush, kissed off my conscience.

Now I just smack your lips and skim
skinned knees when our boy falls.
When I sleep alone, I recall your hand
cupping my cheek, the house spinning

as we stood dizzy in our first kiss.
Sweetheart, let's find that blazing space
again—what we named love—
and seal it hand to hand, lip to lip.

—*Christine Stewart-Nuñez*

Sycophant's Guide to Ass-kissing

If you've kissed one, my friend, and think you've kissed
them all, don't kid yourself. They're everywhere.
So study them awhile before you waste
your sweetness on a worthless derrière.

But once you've made a viable selection,
don't hesitate to play it to the max—
an earnest smile, a hint of genuflection
will tame the cockiest of egomaniacs

and turn them into pussycats, who preen
and simper at the very thought of basking
in your balderdash. It's time to claim
your sweet reward—it's yours, just for the asking.

No reason in the world to feel inferior
while osculating someone's fat posterior.

—*Marilyn L. Taylor*

Men Kissing

Men kissing, men kissing men in a movie,
women kissing, kissing women in the next,
then men kissing women, women, men,

lips swelling into sexual pout,
tongues like petals in storm whorling
on a screen in the basement

of the Methodist Church. Not porn, not instruction
but an ancient lesson—adoration,
how the mouth without words is made holy.

In the diner after the movies, men kissing,
a blonde and a redhead. Over rhubarb pie and coffee
I'm imagining the redhead kissing me.

It's good, as good as any lover,
lips so full I want to gloss them with crimson,
signaling to ruin, *Pass over here.*

In the shiny metal wall, I glimpse a smeary face,
my own, blurred enough it could be my brother's
leaning toward our father, ready for a bedtime kiss.

My brother, little, kissing our father,
my brother, grown, kissing our father.
Every night of the life they lived together,

Father leaning back in the rocker, tilting his head,
his mouth toward his son, Son leaning down,
thin lips pursed, his nose, so like Mother's,

brushing Father's nose, his stubbled chin
brushing Father's stubbled chin,
the two of them, homophobic and affectionate,

saying goodnight with a kiss as soft
as the first kiss of the men in the movie, the men
in the diner, soft as kisses I have given or received.

—*J. C. Todd*

Walk in a Winter Storm

The snow is flinging pelts that cling
so all the wooded trees look birch,
everything wet-headed with the kiss
of masking flakes. Columns of trunks cut
in half in blinking white. We lumber
round the open field in padded coats
and boots among the fallen, numbed limbs.
It's witching hour, striking winter's four.
Who has a better way of showing something
new, covering the past, sweeping clean
a room. Who kisses and asks for nothing
in return? Today, inside my body
in the house I sat, stuck between four walls.
Until you called and said, come love the storm.

—*Sharon Tracey*

The Kiss of Death

is a family kiss, blood to blood,
Michael Coreleone
gripping brother Fredo
by the chops
and planting a big one
to signify the ancient meaning:
"You're a dead man/
I love you,"
the original mixed message,
passed branch to branch
up the family weeping willow
since Cain and Absalom,

like the last kiss
I gave my father,
lightly on his forehead
as he lay gowned and diapered
in his last room, his skin
damp, his mind cornered
by something bad come round
to grill him every waking hour,

maybe by the dream I had,
where I finally threw a punch,
then kept it up till I snapped
awake,

or maybe by a dream he had
about *his* father, that mostly-
loving man he said would sometimes

flail him with a razor strop
—once till Grandma screamed—
and kiss him afterwards.
My father taught himself
to flail with words
and silences. His kisses stabbed.

"I love you, Dad," I lied
to no one in particular before I left,
wiping off the blade,
meaning every word.

—*William Trowbridge*

Open Door

It happened in a doorway, a surprise,
an opening into a beginning, into
a stage in becoming. Sixteen years
piled outside, ready for forgetting.
I forgot to close my eyes. She was
every small thing I knew to want:
voice, humor, talent, nearness,
strong with her hands wrapped—
I don't recall her hands, actually,
though I held them when no one
could see. She had a boyfriend
that wasn't me. We shared a few
afternoons, our kisses becoming
like baseball cards, vestiges of some
rapidly disappearing, simplistic now.
The last ended on a street corner
where I said, "See you later," and that
turned out truer than I meant it to be.
Sometimes, I can still feel the jamb and
my mouth pressed wide, can still see
her eyes opening, finally, to meet mine.

—*David Vincenti*

Germs from Everyone We've Kissed Stay in Our Mouths Until We Die

—Guest on *Oprah*

That must be why I don't forget the day I left my turtle
on his back in the sun, and Mom found me
kissing his shell, wailing, "Wake up! Please!"

The time my son called his windbreaker a *break-
winder* sparked a kiss that keeps me chuckling today.
As for you, poor, skinny, drug-dazed runaway

who lay on Tim's couch like a paralytic, whimpering,
"I love you," then kept me awake, sobbing,
"Don't go," on a school night—thank God I didn't

lie to you. Though I ducked out "to the bathroom,"
and kept moving till I was home, part of me stayed,
and—as long as you're still living—always will.

—*Charles Harper Webb*

French Lesson, Last Day of Summer Vacation

I never knew a tongue
could do such things.
I was in junior high.
The girl was younger but
more experienced than me.

All afternoon we sat
on her parents' front porch
making out like underwater explorers,
tongues descending through teeth,
around gums, into the caverns
of our adolescent mouths,
coming up only occasionally for air.

I never saw that girl after that
impromptu make-out session.
I don't recall anything about her
other than her name and her tongue:
Sherri with an *i*, not a *y*
like that falsettoed Four Seasons song
I hated, but which served for years
as a reminder of our own twist party.

I returned down the street to Grandma's,
older, for sure, wiser about *Frenching*,
but lingering under the surface
were still more depths to dive into,
deeper, lower.

—*Scott Wiggerman*

Never Say Die

Dear World: I am going to eat you alive.
Swallow you whole. Take you to the cleaners.
Clean you out. Take you for everything you've got.
Get you so hot you'll sigh until your shoes untie.
Never let you go. Never say goodbye. I will cry,
me, a grown man, before I'll say goodbye.
All I want to do is kiss you on the lips, just once
before I go. Okay, maybe touch your face too.
Okay, maybe take your clothes off and lick
every part of you. Okay, maybe make love to
you in the back of the car. Okay okay okay.
I won't die, ever. I won't cry, ever. I won't
try to kiss you, except this one time. I will
sneak a smoke with you. I will sneak a poke
with you, beautiful world, with your green
feminine curvy hills, your blue skies like blue
eyes, your charms, your storms, your amazing
ass, your volcanoes, your cups of coffee,
your plans for the future, your soft bed,
your soft voice, your milk-filled breasts,
your wicked sense of humor. God, I am
so in love with you, and I don't know what
to do, where to turn with this permanent
ache for you, this yearning.
Please don't make me go, okay?
Please don't make me go.

—*Terence Winch*

Blazon

after Breton

My love with his hair of nightingales
With his chest of pigeon flutter, of gray doves preening
    themselves at dawn
With his shoulders of tender balconies half in shadow, half in sun
My love with his long-boned thighs the map of Paris of my tongue
With his ink-stained tongue, his tongue the tip
of a steeple plunged into milky sky
My love with his wishing teeth
With his fingers of nervous whispering, his fingers of a boy
whose toys were cheap and broken easily
My love with his silent thumbs
With his eyes of a window smudged of a train that passes in
    the night
With his nape of an empty rain coat
hung by the collar, sweetly bowed
My love with his laughter of an empty stairwell, rain all afternoon
With his mouth the deepest flower to which
I have ever put my mouth

—Cecilia Woloch

Kissing

Under a pale, pastel, early morning sky,
   webbed indigos and gray-yellows,
Hannah Grebholzer and Harry Fox
   exchanged succulent, yielding kisses.

Necks extended forward, flamingo-like,
   they clutched trig and French books,
While all their teenage being
   simmered in their supple, grappling mouths.

The bus driver we called Ajax—
   a tallow face tattooed with stubble—
Asked aloud if love wasn't grand.
   He rat-a-tatted his fingers on the wheel

And hummed a concoction he called swing.
   Minutes elapsed that were more
Than millennia. Oh kisses were overripe apples;
   fondled scents; plush instincts

Of the warm, exhaling earth; exclamatory
   sighs distended into weak-kneed moans,
As if mortals balanced the maculate tension
   of passion like a globe that is still, and spins.

—*Baron Wormser*

A Girl I Kissed When I Was Sixteen

1967, the summer of love

She had this way, at the end of a kiss,
or between kisses, of running her tongue
light and wet around my lips,
a slow circumference along

the open hungry mouth of me.
Every time it made me shiver
and lurch, involuntarily quiver,
even shudder. She thought it was funny

and smiled, so that when we resumed
kissing, I was kissing her smile,
which meant another kind of thrill.
We were in the rumpus room,

her parents' basement. Pool table,
pinball machine, fridge full of beer.
I wasn't encouraged to do anymore,
just kiss her and hold her. If I'd been able

to, I would've. I wanted to, I know,
but I was so lost, other stuff
didn't matter. It was enough,
kissing, her licking my lips just so.

—*Robert Wrigley*

Kiss Scar

We tore off wedges of injera from the bread bowl,
scooping up doro or key wat and shiro.
My first time eating Ethiopian food, I was

enticed by the tingle of spice on lips and tongue,
how it mingled lavishly with sips of mead,
with hunger for the unknown, a piquant unwrapping

in the mouth. It was after class and a way for us
to relish our taste for poets and rhythms, our shared
interest in savory linguistics. After the meal,

we continued to the couch in your apartment,
where I couldn't stop studying your scarred upper lip
as you spoke, a hook through cupid's bow

like the wound of a fish that broke free,
trace of a past that flavored you more succulent.
Partial to seafood, I imagined your lips would taste

like a delectable, spiced morsel, a portion of
that bread of life dipped in saucy experience.
Your shoulder arched my way as if to say

catch me, the loose folds of your blouse
almost scaling themselves. But I couldn't pluck up
the courage even to touch your hand. Such

a green fisherman, I sailed off that night
with empty nets, not even a peck to hold us over
to the next dinner that never came. The lines

that drew us in that night snapped, and we drifted,
farther from each other than either of us could reach.
And to this day, I hunger for that exotic dish.

—*Michael T. Young*

Kissing the Long Face of a Greyhound

My dog's head is the exact shape and size
of a Brooks leather bicycle saddle,
and I love to seat a kiss
on the snout of her,
bending over that jetty of face,
our heads cheekbone to cheekbone—
if a hound can be found to have cheeks—
feel the velvet of that peninsula on my lips,
the faint scent of grime and grass,
the ghost of a tongue trail
grazing her platinum fur.
The thrill of knowing we are only
the span of a sense memory
from past perfidy,
a whisker's breadth
from pointed tooth and unfurling flesh.

—*Yvonne Zipter*

Contributors

Kim Addonizio has authored twelve books of poetry, fiction, and non-fiction, most recently a memoir, *Bukowski in a Sundress: Confessions from a Writing Life* (Penguin, 2016), and *Mortal Trash: Poems* (W. W. Norton, 2016). Her collection, *Tell Me,* was a National Book Award Finalist. She has received NEA and Guggenheim fellowships and two Pushcart Prizes. She teaches poetry workshops online and in California.

Kelli Russell Agodon is the author of *Hourglass Museum* (White Pine P, 2014), a finalist for both the Washington State Book Awards and the Julie Suk Poetry Prize. Her second book, *Letters from the Emily Dickinson Room,* won the Foreword Indies Book of the Year Award for poetry. She is the co-founder of Two Sylvias Press where she works as editor and book cover designer. She lives in Seattle.

Susan Aizenberg is the author of three poetry collections, most recently *Quiet City* (BkMk P, 2015). She was also co-editor with Erin Belieu of *The Extraordinary Tide: New Poetry by American Women* (Columbia UP, 2001). She lives in Iowa City, where she teaches in the Iowa Summer Writing Festival.

Nin Andrews is the author of seven chapbooks and seven full-length poetry collections, most recently *The Last Orgasm* (Etruscan P, 2019). Her poems have appeared in *Ploughshares, Agni, The Paris Review*, and four editions of *Best American Poetry*.

Wendy Barker's sixth collection, *One Blackbird at a Time* (BkMk P, 2015), received the John Ciardi Prize for Poetry. Her fifth chapbook, *Shimmer,* was published by Glass Lyre Press in 2019. Her poems have appeared in numerous journals and anthologies, including *The Best American Poetry 2013*. Recipient of NEA and Rockefeller fellowships, she teaches at the University of Texas at San Antonio.

Tony Barnstone is the author of twenty books, including seven books of poetry, most recently *Pulp Sonnets*. He is also a distinguished translator of Chinese literature and editor of world literature textbooks. His awards include The Poets Prize, a Pushcart Prize, and fellowships from the NEA, the NEH, and the California Arts Council. He teaches at Whittier College.

Tina Barry is the author of *Mall Flower: Poems and Short Fiction* (Big Table Publishing, 2015). She also wrote and curated "The Virginia Project," a traveling written word and visual arts collaboration (2018-2019). Her writing appears in *Drunken Boat, Connotation Press,* and the *Nasty Women Poets*. She is a teaching artist at The Poetry Barn and Gemini Ink.

Ellen Bass is the author of three poetry books, most recently *Like a Beggar* (Copper Canyon, 2014). Her poetry has appeared in *The New Yorker, The American Poetry Review,* and elsewhere. Her awards include fellowships from the NEA and the California Arts Council, three Pushcart Prizes, the Lambda Literary Award, and the Pablo Neruda Prize. A Chancellor of the Academy of American Poets, she teaches in the MFA writing program at Pacific University.

Michele Battiste is the author of three poetry collections, most recently *Waiting for the Wreck to Burn*, which received the 2018 Louise Bogan Award from Trio House Press. She is also the author of several chapbooks, including *Left: Letters to Strangers* (Grey Book P, 2014). She lives in Colorado.

Jane Beal has published several collections of poetry, most recently *Journey* (Origami Poems, 2019). Her chapbook, *Sanctuary*, was nominated for the Conference on Christianity and Literature's Award in Belles Lettres. She has also produced "The Jazz Bird," an audio recording project combining music and poetry. She teaches at the University of La Verne in California.

Jan Beatty is the author of five full-length books, most recently *Jackknife: New and Selected Poems* (U of Pittsburgh P, 2017), winner of the 2018 Paterson Prize. Her earlier book, *Mad River*, won the Agnes Lynch Starrett award. She is managing editor of MadBooks, a small press for books and chapbooks by women. She also directs the creative writing program at Carlow University and is Co-Director of the MFA program.

Jeanne Marie Beaumont is the author of four books of poetry, including *Letters from Limbo* and the National Poetry Series winner, *Placebo Effects*. Her play, *Asylum Song*, was presented Off Broadway in New York in 2019. She has taught for Rutgers University, The Frost Place, and the Unterberg Poetry Center of the 92nd Street Y.

Margo Berdeshevsky is the author of four collections, most recently *Before the Drought* (Glass Lyre P, 2017), a finalist for the National Poetry Series. She is a past recipient of the Robert H. Winner Award from the Poetry

Society of America. Her work has appeared in *Poetry International, New Letters, The Kenyon Review,* and elsewhere. She lives in Paris.

Jacqueline Berger's fourth book, *The Day You Miss Your Exit,* was published in 2018 by Broadstone Press. Several of her poems have been featured on Garrison Keillor's *The Writer's Almanac.* She teaches at Notre Dame de Namur University in Belmont, California.

Michelle Bitting is the author of four collections of poetry, most recently *Broken Kingdom* which won the 2018 Catamaran Prize. Her poems have appeared in *The American Poetry Review, Narrative, Green Mountains Review,* and elsewhere. She is a Lecturer in Poetry and Creative Writing Studies at Loyola Marymount University.

Julie E. Bloemeke is the author of *Slide to Unlock* (Sibling Rivalry, 2020), her debut collection. Her poetry has appeared in *Prairie Schooner, Gulf Coast, Crab Orchard Review,* and elsewhere. Her work has also appeared in *Nasty Women Poets* and *The Writer's Chronicle.* She is a graduate of the Bennington Writing Seminars.

Laure-Anne Bosselaar is the author of four collections of poetry, most recently *These Many Rooms* (Four Way Books, 2019). Her earlier book, *Small Gods of Grief,* won the Isabella Gardner Prize for Poetry. She is the Santa Barbara Poet Laureate (2019-2021), recipient of a Pushcart Prize, editor of four anthologies, and a faculty member in the Low Residency MFA program at Pine Manor College in Boston.

Elya Braden took a long detour from her creative endeavors to pursue an eighteen-year career as a corporate lawyer and entrepreneur. She is now a writer and collage artist living in Los Angeles. Her work has been published in *Gyroscope, Rattle, Willow Review,* and elsewhere.

Jason Lee Brown is the author of the novel *Prowler: The Mad Gasser of Mattoon,* a novella, and a poetry chapbook. His writing has also appeared in such journals as *The Kenyon Review, North American Review,* and *The Journal.* He is editor-in-chief of *River Styx* literary magazine and series editor of *New Stories from The Midwest.*

Kurt Brown (1944-2013) authored six collections of poetry. His posthumous *New & Selected: I've Come This Far to Say Hello* was published by Tiger Bark Press in 2014. He was also the author of a book of essays on poetry, *The Blind Man's Elephant* (2019), and the editor of ten anthologies. He taught at Sarah Lawrence College and at UC Santa Barbara.

Debra Bruce's most recent book is *Survivors' Picnic* (Word Press, 2012). Her poems have been published in such journals as *The Cincinnati Review, Mezzo Cammin, Poetry,* and *Women's Studies Quarterly*. She is Professor Emeritus at Northeastern Illinois University and lives in Chicago.

Jennifer Burd is the author of two books of poetry, most recently *Days Late Blue* (Cherry Grove, 2017) and a chapbook, *Receiving the Shore*. She is also author of a book of creative nonfiction, *Daily Bread: A Portrait of Homeless Men & Women* (Bottom Dog, 2009). She teaches online creative writing classes through The Loft Literary Center in Minneapolis.

Elena Karina Byrne is the author of three books of poetry, most recently *Squander* (Omnidawn, 2016). She is a freelance professor and editor, as well as the Poetry Consultant & Moderator for the Los Angeles Times Festival of Books and the Literary Programs Director for the Ruskin Art Club. Her publications include the *Pushcart Prize XXXIII, Best American Poetry, Poetry,* and *The Kenyon Review*.

Lauren Camp is the author of four poetry collections, most recently *Turquoise Door* (3: A Taos P, 2018). Her third book, *One Hundred Hungers* (Tupelo P, 2016), won the Dorset Prize and was a finalist for the Arab American Book Award and the Housatonic Book Award. Her poems have appeared in *The Los Angeles Review, New England Review, The Cortland Review,* and elsewhere. She lives and teaches in New Mexico.

Neil Carpathios is the author of five full-length poetry collections, most recently *Confessions of a Captured Angel* (Terrapin Books, 2016) and *Far Out Factoid* (FutureCycle P, 2017). He also edited the anthology *Every River on Earth: Writing from Appalachian Ohio* (Ohio UP, 2014). He is an associate professor of English and Creative Writing at Shawnee State University in Ohio.

Robin Rosen Chang has had poems published in *Cream City Review, Michigan Quarterly Review, North American Review,* and elsewhere. The recipient of the Poet's Choice Award in the Oregon Poetry Association's Fall 2018 Poetry Contest, she earned an MFA in Poetry from Warren Wilson College. An ESL teacher, she lives in NJ.

Amanda Chiado is the author of the chapbook *Vitiligod: The Ascension of Michael Jackson* (Dancing Girl P, 2016). Her poetry and flash fiction have been published in *Sequestrum, Best New Poets, Cimarron Review,* and elsewhere. She works for the San Benito County Arts Council, is a California Poet in the Schools, and edits for Jersey Devil Press.

Christopher Citro is the author of *The Maintenance of the Shimmy-Shammy* (Steel Toe Books, 2015). His awards include a 2019 fellowship from the Ragdale Foundation and a 2018 Pushcart Prize. His poems appear in such journals as *Ploughshares, Crazyhorse, The Missouri Review,* and *Alaska Quarterly Review.* He is poetry editor for *decomP.* He teaches creative writing at SUNY Oswego and lives in Syracuse, New York.

Patricia Clark is the author of five volumes of poetry, most recently *The Canopy* (Terrapin Books, 2017). She has also published three chapbooks, including *Deadlifts* (New Michigan P, 2018). Her poems have appeared in *North American Review, Alaska Quarterly Review, New Letters,* and elsewhere.

Cathryn Cofell is the author of *Sister Satellite* (Cowfeather P, 2013), several chapbooks, and a poetry/music CD. Her awards include the Lorine Niedecker Prize. She helped launch the Wisconsin Poet Laureate Commission, the literary journal *Verse Wisconsin*, the Wisconsin Fellowship of Poetry Chapbook Prize, and the Poetry Unlocked reading series.

Geraldine Connolly is the author of four poetry collections, most recently *Aileron* (Terrapin Books, 2018). She has taught at the Writers Center in Maryland, Chautauqua Institution, and the University of Arizona Poetry Center. She has received fellowships from the NEA, Maryland Arts Council, and Bread Loaf Writers' Conference. She lives in Tucson, Arizona.

Jackie Craven is the author of *Secret Formulas & Techniques of the Masters* (Brick Road Poetry P, 2018). Her chapbook, *Our Lives Became Unmanageable* (Omnidawn), won the publisher's award for Fabulist Fiction. She has poems in *The Massachusetts Review, New Ohio Review, River Styx,* and elsewhere. She completed her Doctor of Arts in Writing from the University at Albany.

Jim Daniels' poetry books include *Rowing Inland* (Wayne State UP, 2017), *Street Calligraphy* (Steel Toe Books, 2017), and *The Middle Ages* (Red Mountain P, 2018). He is also the author of six collections of fiction, including *The Perp Walk* (Michigan State UP, 2019), and has edited six anthologies, including *Respect: The Poetry of Detroit Music* (Michigan State UP, 2020).

Jessica de Koninck is the author of one full-length collection, *Cutting Room* (Terrapin Books, 2016), and one chapbook, *Repairs.* Her work has appeared in *Diode, Mom Egg Review,* and *Poetry Magazine* and has twice been featured on *Verse Daily*. A resident of Montclair, NJ, and a retired attorney, she serves on the editorial board of *Jewish Currents* magazine.

Maureen Doallas is the author of *Neruda's Memoirs: Poems* (T. S. Poetry P, 2011). She has published poems in *The Found Poetry Review, Rattle Poets Respond*, and other journals. Her work has also been anthologized in *Alice in Wonderland, Water's Edge,* and *Two Dreamers*. She is the editor of "Artist Watch" for the online arts magazine *Escape Into Life*.

Lynn Domina is the author of two poetry collections, most recently *Framed in Silence* (Main Street Rag, 2011). She is also the editor of *Poets on the Psalms* (Trinity UP, 2008). Her work appears in *St. Ann's Review, The Kenyon Review, Valparaiso Poetry Review,* and elsewhere. She serves as Head of the English Department at Northern Michigan University and is the creative writing editor of *The Other Journal*.

Caitlin Doyle's work has appeared in *The Atlantic, The Guardian, The Yale Review,* and elsewhere. Her work has also been featured on *Poetry Daily*, the Poetry Foundation's *Poem of the Day* series, and *American Life in Poetry*. She has received awards and fellowships from the Yaddo Colony, the MacDowell Colony, and the Bread Loaf Writers' Conference. She is a former Associate Editor of *The Cincinnati Review*.

Denise Duhamel is the author of several books of poetry, most recently *Scald* (U of Pittsburgh P, 2017). She and Julie Marie Wade co-authored *The Unrhymables: Collaborations in Prose* (Noctuary P, 2019). She is a Distinguished University Professor in the MFA program at Florida International University in Miami.

Jane Ebihara is the author of two chapbooks, *A Reminder of Hunger and Wings* (Finishing Line P, 2019) and *A Little Piece of Mourning* (Finishing Line P, 2014). Her poems have appeared in *U.S. 1 Worksheets, Edison Literary Review, Adanna,* and elsewhere. She lives in NJ.

Alexis Rhone Fancher is the author of four poetry collections, most recently *Junkie Wife* (Moon Tide P, 2018). She is also the author of a chapbook, *The Dead Kid Poems* (2019). Her work has appeared in *Best American Poetry, Plume, Rattle, Diode,* and elsewhere. She is poetry editor of *Cultural Weekly*.

Ann Fisher-Wirth is the author of six books of poems, most recently *The Bones of Winter Birds* (Terrapin Books, 2019). A senior fellow of the Black Earth Institute, she has had senior Fulbrights to Switzerland and

Sweden and was Poet-in-Residence at Randolph College in 2017. She teaches at the University of Mississippi and directs the Environmental Studies program.

Alice Friman is the author of seven collections of poetry, most recently *Blood Weather* (LSU, 2019). She won the 2012 Georgia Author of the Year Award in Poetry for her book *Vinculum*. She is the recipient of a Pushcart Prize and the 2016 Paumanok Award. Professor Emerita of English and creative writing at the University of Indianapolis, she lives in Georgia, where she was Poet-in-Residence at Georgia College.

Deborah Gerrish is the author of two books of poetry, most recently *Light in Light* (Wipf and Stock, 2017), and a chapbook. Her poems appear in *The Crafty Poet* and *The Practicing Poet*. She received an Edward Fry Fellowship from Rutgers University and holds an MFA in Poetry from Drew University. She teaches poetry workshops at Fairleigh Dickinson University and resides in NJ.

Ona Gritz is the author of *Geode*, a finalist for the 2013 Main Street Rag Poetry Book Award. With her husband Daniel Simpson, she is co-author of *Border Songs: A Conversation in Poems* (Finishing Line P, 2017) and co-editor of *More Challenges for the Delusional* (Diode Editions, 2018). Her poems have appeared in *Ploughshares*, *Bellevue Literary Review*, *Seneca Review*, and elsewhere.

Bruce Guernsey is the author of *From Rain: Poems, 1970-2010* (Ecco Qua P, 2012). His poems have appeared in *Poetry, The Atlantic, Triquarterly*, and elsewhere. His awards include fellowships from the NEA, Bread Loaf Writers' Conference, and McDowell Colony. He has been a Fulbright Senior Lecturer in American Poetry in Portugal and Greece and is Distinguished Professor of English Emeritus, Eastern Illinois University.

Tami Haaland is the author of three poetry collections, most recently *What Does Not Return* (Lost Horse P, 2018). Her first collection, *Breath in Every Room*, won the Nicholas Roerich First Book Award. Her work has been featured on *The Writer's Almanac, Verse Daily*, and *American Life in Poetry*. She served as Montana's Poet Laureate (2013-2015) and teaches at Montana State University.

Jared Harél is the author of the poetry collection *Go Because I Love You* (Diode Editions, 2018). His awards include the Stanley Kunitz Memorial Prize from *The American Poetry Review*, the William Matthews Poetry Prize from *Asheville Poetry Review,* and two Individual Artist Grants from Queens Council on the Arts. His poems have appeared in *32 Poems, Massachusetts Review, The Southern Review,* and elsewhere. He lives in Queens, NY.

Jeffrey Harrison is the author of five full-length books of poetry, most recently *Into Daylight* (Tupelo P, 2014), which won the Dorset Prize. His awards include four Pushcart Prizes and fellowships from the Guggenheim Foundation, the NEA, and the Bogliasco Foundation. His poems have been featured on *The Writer's Almanac, American Life in Poetry, Best American Poetry,* and *Poetry Daily*.

Hunt Hawkins is the author of *The Domestic Life* (U of Pittsburgh P), which received the 1994 Agnes Lynch Starrett Poetry Prize from the University of Pittsburgh Press. His poems have appeared in *The Georgia Review, Poetry, TriQuarterly,* and elsewhere. He teaches at the University of South Florida.

Shayla Hawkins is the author of *Carambola* (David Robert Books, 2012). Her work has appeared in *The Caribbean Writer, Taj Mahal Review,* the *Encyclopedia of African American Women Writers,* and elsewhere. She is a founding fellow and graduate of the Cave Canem Workshop and has been a featured reader at the Geraldine R. Dodge Poetry Festival and the Library of Congress. She lives in Michigan.

Karen Paul Holmes has two poetry collections, most recently *No Such Thing as Distance* (Terrapin Books, 2018). She was named a 2016 Best Emerging Poet by Stay Thirsty Media. Her publications include *Prairie Schooner, Valparaiso Review,* and *Poet Lore.* She founded and hosts a critique group in Atlanta and Writers' Night Out in the Blue Ridge Mountains.

John Hoppenthaler's most recent of his three books is *Domestic Garden* (Carnegie Mellon, 2015). With Kazim Ali, he co-edited a volume of essays and interviews on the poetry of Jean Valentine, *This-World Company* (U Michigan P, 2012). He edits "A Poetry Congeries" for *Connotation Press,* is on the advisory board for Backbone Press, and teaches at East Carolina University.

Karla Huston served as the Wisconsin Poet Laureate (2017-2018). She is the author of *A Theory of Lipstick* (Main Street Rag, 2013) as well as eight chapbooks, including *Grief Bone* (Five Oaks P, 2017). The recipient of a 2012 Pushcart Prize, she teaches poetry writing at The Mill: A Place for Writers in Wisconsin.

Gray Jacobik is the author of six books of poetry, most recently *Eleanor* (CavanKerry, 2020). Awards for her earlier books include the Juniper Prize, the X. J. Kennedy Prize, the AWP Poetry Series Award, and the 2016 William Meredith Award in Poetry. Her poems have appeared in *The Kenyon Review, Poetry, The Georgia Review, Ploughshares,* and elsewhere. She is University Professor Emerita from Eastern Connecticut State University.

Richard Jones is the author of seven books from Copper Canyon Press, most recently *Stranger on Earth* (2018). He is the editor of *Poetry East* and its many anthologies, such as *London, The Last Believer in Words,* and *Bliss.* He also edits the free worldwide poetry app, "The Poet's Almanac."

Allison Joseph is the author of several collections of poems, including *Confessions of a Barefaced Woman* (Red Hen P, 2018), a finalist for the Paterson Poetry Prize and a nominated work for the NAACP Image Award in Poetry. She is on the faculty at Southern Illinois University where she directs the MFA Program in Creative Writing and co-edits *Crab Orchard Review.*

Tina Kelley is the author of four poetry collections, most recently *Abloom & Awry* (CavanKerry, 2017) and *Rise Wildly* (CavanKerry, 2020). *Ardor* won the Jacar Press 2017 chapbook competition. She also co-authored *Almost Home: Helping Kids Move from Homelessness to Hope.* Her writing has appeared in *Poetry East, Prairie Schooner,* and *The Best American Poetry 2009.*

Adele Kenny is the author of several collections of poetry, most recently *A Lightness, A Thirst, or Nothing at All* (Welcome Rain, 2015), a Paterson Poetry Prize finalist. She is founding director of the Carriage House Poetry Series and poetry editor for *Tiferet.* Her awards include poetry fellowships from the NJ State Council on the Arts and Kean University's Distinguished Alumni Award.

Claire Keyes is the author of two books of poems, most recently *What Diamonds Can Do* (WordTech, 2015) and a chapbook, *Rising and Falling.* Her poems have appeared in *Whale Road Review, Comstock Review,* and *Crab Orchard Review,* and have been featured on *The Writer's Almanac.* Professor Emerita at Salem State University, she lives in Massachusetts, where she conducts the Poetry Salon at Abbot Public Library.

David Kirby is the author of several collections of poetry, including *Get Up, Please* (LSU P, 2016) and *The House on Boulevard St.: New and Selected*

Poems, a finalist for the National Book Award in 2007. His honors include Pushcart Prizes, fellowships from the NEA and the Guggenheim Foundation, and a 2016 Lifetime Achievement Award from the Florida Humanities Council.

Lynne Knight is the author of six full-length poetry collections, including *The Language of Forgetting* (Sixteen Rivers, 2018) and *The Persistence of Longing* (Terrapin Books, 2016). Her work has appeared in such journals as *The Kenyon Review, Poetry,* and *The Southern Review.* Her honors include publication in *Best American Poetry*, a Poetry Society of America award, and an NEA grant. She lives on Vancouver Island.

Danusha Laméris is the author of *Bonfire Opera* (U of Pittsburgh P, 2010) and *The Moons of August* (Autumn House P, 2014), which won the Autumn House Press poetry prize and was a finalist for the Milt Kessler Book Award. Her poems have been published in *The Best American Poetry, The New York Times, The American Poetry Review,* and elsewhere. She is the Poet Laureate of Santa Cruz County, California.

Lance Larsen, former poet laureate of Utah, has published five poetry collections, most recently *What the Body Knows* (Tampa, 2018). He has received a Pushcart Prize and fellowships from Ragdale, Sewanee, and the NEA. Six of his essays have been listed as notables in *Best American Essays*. He teaches English at BYU where he serves as department chair.

Dorianne Laux's most recent collection is *Only As the Day Is Long: New and Selected* (W. W. Norton, 2019). She is also the author of *The Book of Men*, winner of the Paterson Poetry Prize, and *Facts about the Moon*, winner of the Oregon Book Award. She teaches poetry at North Carolina State and Pacific University.

Jenifer Browne Lawrence is the author of *Grayling* (Perugia P, 2015) and *One Hundred Steps from Shore* (Blue Begonia P, 2006). Her awards include the Perugia Press Prize, the Orlando Poetry Prize, and the James Hearst Poetry Prize. Her work has appeared in *The Cincinnati Review, Narrative, Los Angeles Review*, and elsewhere. She edits *Crab Creek Review*.

Lynn Levin is the author of seven books, including the poetry collection *Miss Plastique* (Ragged Sky P, 2013). Her poems have appeared in *The Hopkins Review, Artful Dodge, Mezzo Cammin*, and in such anthologies as *Nasty Women Poets* and *Rabbit Ears*. She teaches at Drexel University.

Jeffrey Levine's most recent book is *At the Kinnegad Home for the Bewildered* (Salmon P, 2019). He is also the principal translator of *Canto General*, Pablo Neruda's epic work. His poetry prizes include the Larry Levis Prize, the James Hearst Poetry Prize, and the *Mississippi Review* Poetry Prize. A graduate of the Warren Wilson MFA Program for Writers, he is the founder and publisher of Tupelo Press.

Katharyn Howd Machan is the author of several collections of poetry, most recently *Selected Poems* (FutureCycle P, 2018) and *What the Piper Promised,* winner of the 2018 AQP chapbook competition. Selected as Tompkins County's first poet laureate, she is a professor in the Department of Writing at Ithaca College.

Marjorie Maddox has published eleven collections of poetry, most recently *True, False, None of the Above* (Cascade Books, 2016). She is also the author of the short story collection *What She Was Saying* (Fomite P) and several children's books. She is assistant editor of the journal *Presence* and teaches English and Creative Writing at Lock Haven University.

Jennifer Maier is the author of two poetry books, most recently *Now, Now* (U of Pittsburgh P, 2013). Her first book, *Dark Alphabet* (Southern Illinois UP), was a finalist for the 2008 Poets' Prize. Her work has appeared in *Plume, The Gettysburg Review, Poetry,* and elsewhere. She teaches at Seattle Pacific University, where she serves as Writer-in-Residence and Associate Editor of *Image.*

Charlotte Mandel's eleventh book of poetry is *Alive and in Use: Poems in the Japanese Form of Haibun* (Kelsay Books, 2019). Her awards include the New Jersey Poets Prize and two fellowships in poetry from the NJ State Council on the Arts. Her critical essays include a series on the role of cinema in the life and work of H. D.

Kelly McQuain is the author of *Velvet Rodeo,* which won the 2014 Bloom poetry prize. His prose, poetry, and illustrations have appeared in *The Pinch, Painted Bride Quarterly, The Philadelphia Inquirer,* and elsewhere. He has been a Sewanee Tennessee Williams Scholar and a Lambda Literary Fellow, and has received two fellowships from the Pennsylvania Council on the Arts.

Natasha Moni is the author of a full-length collection, *The Cardiologist's Daughter* (Two Sylvias P, 2014), and three chapbooks. Her poetry, essays, fiction, and book reviews have been published in such journals as *The Rumpus, Entropy*, and *Diagram*. A 2018 Jack Straw Writer, she lives in Washington State.

Ruth Mota has had poems in such journals as *The Monterey Poetry Review, Caesura,* and *Phren-Z Magazine*. After a career in Public Health, she is now retired and living in the Santa Cruz Mountains of California, where she devotes herself to poetry and leads poetry circles for veterans and men in jail.

Peter E. Murphy is the author of ten books and chapbooks, including *Stubborn Child* (Jane Street P, 2005), a finalist for the Paterson Poetry Prize, and *Looking for Thelma*, winner of the inaugural Wilt Nonfiction Chapbook Prize. His essays and poems have appeared in *The Common, Diode, Guernica,* and elsewhere. He is the founder of Murphy Writing of Stockton University in NJ.

Dion O'Reilly's poetry has appeared in *New Ohio Review, New Letters, Sugar House Review,* the *Lambda Literary Anthology,* and elsewhere. She lives in California.

Amy Pence authored the poetry collections *The Decadent Lovely* (Main Street Rag, 2010), *Armor, Amour* (Ninebark P, 2012), and *[It] Incandescent* (Ninebark, 2018), which won the Eyelands Poetry Award in Athens, Greece. She works as a tutor in Atlanta and teaches a poetry writing class at Emory.

Paulann Petersen, Oregon Poet Laureate Emerita (2010-2014), has seven full-length books of poetry, most recently *One Small Sun* (Salmon Poetry, 2019). Her poems have appeared in such journals as *Poetry, The New Republic*, and *Prairie Schooner*, and have been featured on *Poetry Daily*. In 2013 she was Willamette Writers' Distinguished Northwest Writer.

John Poch's fifth book, *Texases*, was published by WordFarm (2019). His poems have appeared in *The Yale Review, Poetry, The New Republic*, and other journals. In 2014, he was a Fulbright Core Scholar to the University of Barcelona. He teaches in the creative writing program at Texas Tech University.

Andrea Potos is the author of nine poetry collections, most recently *Mothershell* (Kelsay Books, 2019). She is also the author of *A Stone to Carry Home* (Salmon Poetry, 2018) and *Arrows of Light* (Iris P, 2017). The recipient of the William Stafford Prize in Poetry from *Rosebud Magazine*, she lives in Wisconsin.

Wanda S. Praisner is the author of six collections of poetry, most recently *To Illuminate the Way* (Aldrich P, 2018). Her awards include a fellowship from the NJ State Council on the Arts and the 2017 New Jersey Poets Prize. Her work has appeared in *Atlanta Review, Lullwater Review,* and *Prairie Schooner.*

Christine Rhein is the author of *Wild Flight* (Texas Tech UP, 2008), winner of the Walt McDonald Poetry Prize. Her poems have appeared in such journals as *The Gettysburg Review, Michigan Quarterly Review,* and *The Southern Review.* Her work has been featured in *Poetry Daily, Best New Poets,* and *The Best American Nonrequired Reading 2017.* A former automotive engineer, she lives in Michigan.

Susan Rich is the author of four books of poetry, most recently *Cloud Pharmacy* (White Pine P, 2014). Her awards include a PEN USA Award, a Fulbright Fellowship, and a *Times Literary Supplement* Award. Her poems have appeared in the *Antioch Review, New England Review, O Magazine, Pleiades,* and elsewhere. She lives in Seattle.

Susanna Rich is the author of four poetry collections, most recently *Beware the House* (The Poet's P, 2019). She is a Budapest Fulbright Fellow and founding producer, principal writer, and performer at Wild Nights Productions. The recipient of the Presidential Excellence Award for Distinguished Teaching, she is professor of English Studies at Kean University in NJ.

Katherine Riegel is the author of three books of poetry, most recently *Love Songs from the End of the World* (Main Street Rag, 2019) and the chapbook *Letters to Colin Firth.* Her work has appeared in *The Gettysburg Review, Orion, Tin House,* and elsewhere. She is co-founder and poetry editor of *Sweet Lit.*

Kenneth Ronkowitz's poetry has been anthologized in *The Paradelle, The Practicing Poet,* and *The Crafty Poet.* His work has also appeared in such journals as *Tiferet, Lips,* and *Paterson Literary Review,* and has been featured on *The Writer's Almanac.* A former teacher, he has edited PoetsOnline.org since 1998.

Dan Rosenberg is the author of *cadabra* (Carnegie Mellon UP, 2015) and *The Crushing Organ* (Dream Horse P, 2012), winner of the *American Poetry Journal* Book Prize. His poems have appeared in *Ploughshares, Colorado Review,* and *Alaska Quarterly Review.* He teaches literature and creative writing at Wells College in NY.

Susan Rothbard's poetry has appeared in the *The Cortland Review, The Literary Review, Poet Lore, National Poetry Review*, and other journals. Her work has been featured in Ted Kooser's *American Life in Poetry* and on *Verse Daily*. A former high school English teacher, she lives in NJ.

Leigh Camacho Rourks is the author of a collection of short stories, *Moon Trees and Other Orphans* (Black Lawrence P, 2019). Her awards include the St. Lawrence Press Award, the Glenna Luschei *Prairie Schooner* Award, and the Robert Watson *Literary Review* Prize. Her work has appeared in *The Kenyon Review, Prairie Schooner, TriQuarterly*, and elsewhere. She teaches English and Humanities at Beacon College in Florida.

Born in the UK to immigrant parents from Punjab, India, **Rajwant Saghera** completed a BA in English from the University of London. She left the UK and moved to Tanzania, in East Africa, and lived there for seven years, traveling, teaching, and completing a Masters in African Literatures. She now lives in Colombia, in South America, teaching Literature and Theatre.

Nicholas Samaras is the author of two books of poetry, *Hands of the Saddlemaker* (Yale UP, 1992), which received the 1991 Yale Series of Younger Poets Award, and *American Psalm, World Psalm* (Ashland Poetry P, 2014). His awards include fellowships from the NEA and the Lilly Endowment Foundation.

Tim Seibles served as Poet Laureate of Virginia (2016-2018). He is the author of several poetry collections, including *One Turn Around the Sun* (Etruscan P, 2017) and *Fast Animal* (Etruscan P, 2012), a finalist for the 2012 National Book Award and winner of the Theodore Roethke Memorial Prize. He has led workshops for Cave Canem and recently retired from Old Dominion University where he taught in the MFA in Writing program.

Former Poet Laureate of Virginia (2014-2016), **Ron Smith** is the author of four books of poetry, most recently *The Humility of the Brutes* (LSU, 2017). His awards include the Theodore Roethke Poetry Prize from *Poetry Northwest* and the Guy Owen Poetry Prize. His poems have appeared in *The Nation, The Georgia Review, The Kenyon Review*, and elsewhere.

Christine Stewart-Nuñez is the Poet Laureate of South Dakota. She is the author of *Bluewords Greening* (Terrapin Books, 2016), winner of the 2018 Whirling Prize, and three earlier collections. Her awards for creative nonfiction include a Notable Essay in *Best American Essays 2012*. She teaches in the English Department at South Dakota State University.

Marilyn L. Taylor, former Poet Laureate of Wisconsin, is the author of six poetry collections. Her work has appeared in *Poetry, Able Muse, Measure,* and elsewhere. She won the 2016 Margaret Reid Poetry Prize for verse in forms and was a finalist for the X. J. Kennedy Parody Contest and the Howard Nemerov Sonnet award. She is an editor for *Third Wednesday* and *Verse-Virtual.*

J. C. Todd is the author of *What Space This Body* (Wind Publications, 2008) and three chapbooks, most recently *The Damages of Morning* (Moonstone P, 2018), an Eric Hoffer Award finalist. Other awards include the Rita Dove Poetry Prize and fellowships from the Pew Center for Arts & Heritage and the Pennsylvania Council on the Arts. Her poems have appeared in such journals as *The American Poetry Review, Beloit Poetry Journal,* and *The Paris Review.*

Sharon Tracey is the author of the poetry collection *What I Remember Most Is Everything* (All Caps Publishing, 2017). Her poems have appeared in *Common Ground Review, Light: A Journal of Photography and Poetry, Naugatuck River Review,* and elsewhere.

William Trowbridge, Poet Laureate of Missouri from 2012 to 2016, is the author of seven poetry collections, most recently V*anishing Point* (Red Hen P, 2017). His awards include an Academy of American Poets Prize and a Pushcart Prize. His poems have appeared in such journals as *Poetry, The Gettysburg Review,* and *The Georgia Review.* He is a faculty mentor in the University of Nebraska Omaha Low-Residency MFA in writing program.

David Vincenti is the author of *A Measure of this World: Galileo's Dialog with the Universe* and a chapbook, *To the Ones Who Must Be Loved.* His poems have appeared in such journals as *Naugatuck River Review, The Christian Science Monitor,* and *Schuylkill Valley Journal.* His work has also been included in the anthology *Rabbit Ears: TV Poems.*

Charles Harper Webb's latest collection of poems is *Sidebend World* (U of Pittsburgh P, 2018). He is also the author of an essay collection, *A Million MFAs Are Not Enough* (Red Hen P, 2016). Recipient of Whiting and Guggenheim fellowships, he teaches Creative Writing at California State University, Long Beach.

Scott Wiggerman is the author of three books of poetry, most recently *Leaf and Beak: Sonnets* (Purple Flag, 2015), a finalist for the Texas Institute of Letters' Helen C. Smith Memorial Award. He is also the editor of several volumes, including *Wingbeats: Exercises & Practice in*

Poetry (I & II). He lives in Albuquerque, where he chairs the New Mexico State Poetry Society's largest chapter.

Terence Winch is the author of eight poetry collections, most recently *The Known Universe* (Hanging Loose, 2018). His awards include a Columbia Book Award, an American Book Award, an NEA fellowship in poetry, and a Gertrude Stein Award for Innovative Writing. His work is included in such anthologies as the *Oxford Book of American Poetry*, *Poetry 180*, and five editions of *Best American Poetry*.

Cecilia Woloch is the author of six collections of poems and a novel. Her awards include an NEA fellowship, a Fulbright fellowship, and a Pushcart Prize. Her second book, *Tsigan: The Gypsy Poem* (Two Sylvias, 2018, 2nd ed.), has been the basis for multi-media presentations across Europe and the US.

Baron Wormser is the author/co-author of sixteen books and a poetry chapbook. His most recent book is *Legends of the Slow Explosion: Eleven Modern Lives* (Tupelo P, 2018). He has received fellowships from the NEA, Bread Loaf, and the Guggenheim Foundation. From 2000 to 2005 he served as Poet Laureate of Maine.

Robert Wrigley is the author of ten poetry collections, most recently *Box* (Penguin, 2017). His honors include fellowships from the NEA, the Idaho State Commission on the Arts, and the Guggenheim Foundation, as well as the Theodore Roethke Award and two Pushcart Prizes. He is Distinguished Professor Emeritus at the University of Idaho.

Michael T. Young is the author of three full-length collections, most recently *The Infinite Doctrine of Water* (Terrapin Books, 2018). His awards include the Jean Pedrick Chapbook Award for *Living in the Counterpoint* and a fellowship from the NJ State Council on the Arts. His poetry has appeared in *The Comstock Review, One, Rattle,* and *Valparaiso Poetry Review.*

Yvonne Zipter is the author of the full-length collection, *The Patience of Metal* (Hutchinson House, 1990), a Lambda Award Finalist. Her poems have appeared in such journals as *Poetry, Southern Humanities Review,* and *Spoon River Poetry Review.* She is a former manuscript editor at the University of Chicago Press.

Credits

Susan Aizenberg. "Kiss" from *Muse* (Southern Illinois UP). Copyright © 2002 by Susan Aizenberg. Reprinted by permission of the author.

Nin Andrews. "A woman just wants to sleep." Copyright © 2012 by Nin Andrews. First published in *DMQ Review*. Reprinted by permission of the author.

Wendy Barker. "Integration" from *Nothing Between Us* (Del Sol P). Copyright © 2009 by Wendy Barker. Reprinted by permission of the author.

Tony Barnstone. "Nightmare Kiss" from *Sad Jazz: Sonnets* (Sheep Meadow P). Copyright © 2006 by Tony Barnstone. Reprinted by permission of the author.

Tina Barry. "Frida with Monkey." Copyright © 2011 by Tina Barry. First published in *The Prose-Poem Project*. Reprinted by permission of the author.

Ellen Bass. "Gate C22" from *The Human Line*. Copyright © 2007 by Ellen Bass. Reprinted with the permission of The Permissions Company, Inc. on behalf of Copper Canyon Press.

Michele Battiste. "Strategy of a Kiss." Copyright © 2003 by Michele Battiste. First published in *Diagram*. Reprinted by permission of the author.

Jane Beal. "Ariadne Invites Dionysius to Kiss Her" from *After the Labyrinth* (Lulu P). Copyright © 2017 by Jane Beal. Reprinted by permission of the author.

Jan Beatty. "Like Your Grandfather Kisses You" from *Red Sugar* (U of Pittsburgh P). Copyright © 2008 by Jan Beatty. Reprinted by permission of the author.

Jeanne Marie Beaumont. "Good Nothing and Good Night" from *Letters from Limbo*. Copyright © 2016 by Jeanne Marie Beaumont. Reprinted with the permission of The Permissions Company, Inc., on behalf of CavanKerry Press.

Michelle Bitting. "They Are Kissing, in the Pub, Under One." Copyright © 2008 by Michelle Bitting. First published in *Nimrod*. Reprinted by permission of the author.

Laure-Anne Bosselaar. "After Your Shower" in an earlier version from *The Hour Between Dog and Wolf* (BOA Editions). Copyright © 1997 by Laure-Anne Bosselaar. Reprinted by permission of the author.

Elya Braden. "Winning Kiss." Copyright © 2014 by Elya Braden. First published in *Split Lip Magazine*. Reprinted by permission of the author.

Jason Lee Brown. "First Acceptance." Copyright © 2008 by Jason Lee Brown. First published in *Confrontation*. Reprinted by permission of the author.

About the Editor

Diane Lockward is the editor of three poetry craft books, most recently *The Practicing Poet: Writing Beyond the Basics* (Terrapin Books, 2018). She is also the author of four poetry books, most recently *The Uneaten Carrots of Atonement* (Wind Publications, 2016). Her awards include the Quentin R. Howard Poetry Prize, a poetry fellowship from the New Jersey State Council on the Arts, and a Woman of Achievement Award. Her poems have been included in such journals as *Harvard Review, Southern Poetry Review*, and *Prairie Schooner*. Her work has also been featured on *Poetry Daily, Verse Daily, The Writer's Almanac,* and Ted Kooser's *American Life in Poetry*. She is the founder, editor, and publisher of Terrapin Books.

JUL 2019

CPSIA information can be obtained
at www.ICGtesting.com
Printed in the USA
LVHW010852010719
622836LV00002B/437

9 781947 896178